The
Covenant
of
Works

Recovering *our* Confessional Heritage

James M. Renihan, Editor-in-Chief
Richard C. Barcellos, Managing Editor

Arden L. Hodgins, Jr., *A Defense of Confessionalism: Biblical Foundations & Confessional Considerations*

James M. Renihan, *Associational Churchmanship: Second London Confession of Faith 26.12-15*

Richard C. Barcellos, *The Covenant of Works: Its Confessional and Scriptural Basis*

The Covenant of Works
Its Confessional and Scriptural Basis
Richard C. Barcellos

The Institute of Reformed Baptist Studies
Printed by RBAP, Palmdale, CA

Requests for information should be sent to:

RBAP
349 Sunrise Terrace
Palmdale, CA 93551
rb@rbap.net
www.rbap.net

Printed in the United States of America.

Cover design and formatted for print by Cameron Porter. Front cover Confession text was captured and graphically modified from document excerpts at Columbia University Libraries: https://clio.columbia.edu/catalog/4540105.

ISBN-13: 978-0-9916599-6-8
ISBN-10: 0-9916599-6-1

Endorsements

A proper understanding of Adam's state in the garden is fundamental to a coherent doctrine of salvation, which is why this little book on the covenant of works is so important. Richard Barcellos mines the riches of the Reformed Baptist theology and explains the covenant of works with exegetical fidelity and theological clarity. Anyone who wants greater insight into the covenant of works and Reformed Baptist confessional theology should definitely read this book.

J. V. Fesko, Ph.D.
Academic Dean
Professor of Systematic and Historical Theology
Westminster Seminary California
****

No document more amply demonstrates the clear lines of continuity between Reformed Baptist thought and our Christian creedal and Reformed confessional heritage than the Second London Confession of Faith of 1677/1689. And in that Confession we see the biblical teaching on the covenant of works clearly and cogently expressed. It is in breaking that covenant that Adam became a covenant-breaker, and brought down upon us the covenant curse of death (spiritual, physical, and eternal); and it is in keeping that covenant that the Second and Last Adam, our Lord Jesus, became The Covenant Keeper in our place, and brought down to us the covenant blessing of life eternal. I warmly commend the exceptionally fine work represented by this book.

Dr. Liam Goligher
Senior Minister, Tenth Presbyterian Church
Philadelphia, PA
****

Table of Contents

Series Preface

The purpose of the series *Recovering our Confessional Heritage* is to address issues related to the Second London Confession of Faith of 1677/89 (2LCF). This centuries-old Confession is widely recognized as the most important Confession of Faith in Baptist history. First published in England in 1677, it became the standard for Baptists in Colonial America through the publication of the Philadelphia (1742), Ketockton, Virginia (1766), Charleston, South Carolina, Warren, Rhode Island (both 1767), and many other editions of the Confession. As late as 1881, William Cathcart, the editor of *The Baptist Encyclopedia*, could say, "In England and America, churches, individuals, and Associations, with clear minds, with hearts full of love for the truth, . . . have held with veneration the articles of 1689." Since then, it has been adopted by Baptists around the world and translated into many languages.

We believe that, due to two factors, producing a series of short books on the 2LCF will be useful to many pastors and church members. First, there has been increased interest in the 2LCF in the first decade and a half of the twenty-first century. In fact, from the early 1960s, a greater awareness of this Confession among Baptists in the United States and around the world is evident. One of the encouraging proofs of this growing attention is the multiplication of churches who identify the 2LCF as their confessional standard.

Second, there are many issues related to the Confession that need to be clearly and cogently explained in order for an informed and robust recovery of Baptist confessionalism to continue. While churches and individuals have formally adopted the 2LCF as a standard, it has not always been clear that its contents have been fully or properly understood. As a result, the goal of this series is to aid those considering the 2LCF, as well as those already committed to it, in order to produce or maintain an informed and vigorous Baptist confessionalism.

The series will include treatments of various subjects by multiple authors. The subjects to be covered are those the series editors (along with consultants) determine to be of particular interest in our day. The authors will be those who display ample ability to address the issue under discussion. Some of the installments will be more involved than others due to the nature of the subject addressed and perceived current needs. Many of the contributions will cover foundational aspects of the self-consistent theological system expressed in the Confession. Others will address difficult, often misunderstood, or even denied facets of the doctrinal formulations of the 2LCF. Each installment will have a "For Further Reading" bibliography at the end to encourage further study on the issue discussed.

It is hoped that, by the blessing of God, these brief books will produce a better understanding of "the faith which was once for all delivered to the saints" (Jude 3, NKJV) as well as a clearer and more robust understanding of what it means to confess the 2LCF in the twenty-first century.

James M. Renihan, Editor-in-Chief
Richard C. Barcellos, Managing Editor
October 2016

Acknowledgements

The series *Recovering our Confessional Heritage* is sponsored by the Institute of Reformed Baptist Studies in cooperation with Reformed Baptist Academic Press. The Institute of Reformed Baptist Studies is a graduate theological school which aids churches in preparing men to serve in the Gospel Ministry. For more information please visit *irbsseminary.org*.

Most of what is contained in this book will appear in my forthcoming work *Getting the Garden Wrong: A Critique of New Covenant Theology on the Covenant of Works and the Sabbath*. I want to thank Founders Press for permission to use the material for this series.

Richard C. Barcellos, Ph.D.
Grace Reformed Baptist Church
Palmdale, CA

1.

The Covenant of Works: Doctrinal Formulation and Hermeneutics

In order to understand what the 2LCF affirms concerning the doctrine of the covenant of works, it is important to understand how the doctrine was formulated. Knowing what is confessed is important, and knowing how confessional assertions were formulated is as well. This chapter, therefore, focuses on doctrinal formulation and hermeneutics. It may help to introduce a working definition of the covenant of works which will be explained further in subsequent discussion. This definition is offered at this point to identify what the covenant of works asserts in order to show how it was formulated, concentrating on the hermeneutical principles undergirding its formulation. The covenant of works is that divinely sanctioned commitment or relationship God imposed upon Adam in the garden of Eden. Adam was a sinless representative of mankind (i.e., a public person), an image-bearing son of God. This covenant was conditioned upon Adam's obedience, with a penalty for disobedience, all for the bettering of man's state. Here we have the following: 1) sovereign, divine imposition; 2) representation by Adam (i.e., federal headship), a sinless image-bearing son of God; 3) a conditional element (i.e., obedience); 4) a penalty for disobedience (i.e., death); and 5) a promise of reward (i.e., eschatological potential). It is important to keep this definition in mind as we work our way through the discussion.

How the Confessional Doctrine of the Covenant of Works was Formulated

In this section, we will concentrate on how the doctrine of the covenant of works was formulated in the seventeenth century. How this doctrine was *not* formulated will be discussed first.

1. How the doctrine of the covenant of works was not formulated

How was the doctrine of the covenant of works formulated? It was not formulated by the Westminster divines inventing a theory then trying to find it in the Bible, forcing biblical texts into a pre-conceived theological system. The same goes for the Savoy and the Particular Baptist divines. This is essentially what I was told during my seminary days in the late 1980s. The theology of the seventeenth-century divines stood over the Bible as its interpretive lord.

Some think that a theology of the garden was constructed in the minds of men, which included the covenant of works, then a hermeneutic was invented to get there. In other words, an extra-biblical theology led to an extra-biblical hermeneutic, which led to an extra-biblical confessional formulation.[1] Again,

---

[1] Having studied the theological method of seventeenth-century Reformed orthodoxy (especially as it relates to covenant theology and the interpretation of redemptive history), I am convinced from the primary sources that anyone who makes this claim has not read the proper sources, does not understand what they read, or simply does not know what they are talking about, whether they have read the proper sources or not. This claim gives the appearance of being nothing less than a

in this view, their theology and hermeneutical principles stood over the Bible as its interpretive lord.

It should be admitted that the older covenant theologians presupposed a hermeneutic that led to their covenant theology. Let us think through this a bit. If we take theology here to mean what the seventeenth-century covenant theologians said the Bible teaches, and hermeneutics to mean the interpretive principles they *took to the Bible to determine its meaning*, then it is not the case that they presupposed a hermeneutic that led to their theology. It is the case, however, that their theology *and* their hermeneutical principles, though in part distinguishable, were not separate, unrelated categories, one derived from special revelation (i.e., Scripture) and the other exclusively from general revelation (i.e., hermeneutics). In other words, part of their theology (i.e., what they said the Bible taught) was hermeneutics (i.e., the interpretive

---

dismissal tactic. It might carry rhetorical weight with uniformed readers but it has no basis in the facts of history. See Richard C. Barcellos, *The Family Tree of Reformed Biblical Theology: Geerhardus Vos and John Owen – Their Methods of and Contributions to the Articulation of Redemptive History* (Owensboro, KY: RBAP, 2010), 53-107.

principles they utilized to determine what the Bible meant). To be more specific, *their interpretive principles came, in part, from what they believed the Bible said about itself and how it interpreted itself.* They saw texts (i.e., the authors of texts and/or those speaking in the texts) interacting with texts (i.e., authored by others) and further explaining them. They saw texts within Scripture interpreting texts within Scripture, sometimes using words to describe concepts that are not contained in the text being referenced. Recall Acts 2:31, recorded by Luke, where Peter says that David ". . . looked ahead and spoke of the resurrection of the Christ" in Psalm 16. Neither the word "resurrection" nor the word "Christ" occur in the Psalm. Peter is describing *concepts* from Psalm 16 in *words* not used by David in Psalm 16. Later texts can, and do, describe earlier *concepts* with different *words*. In our day, we would say they saw inner-biblical exegesis occurring in the Bible; that is, they saw later texts interpreting and applying earlier texts, and they accounted for it in the way they understood other texts. In other words, they did not impose a wholesale extra-biblical theory of hermeneutics upon the Bible, thus producing their covenant theology. Their hermeneutical process sought to reflect what

Doctrinal Formulation and Hermeneutics

they saw transpiring in the Bible, and in this sense came from Scripture itself, not some extra-biblical source.

This leads to our next question: How was the doctrine of the covenant of works formulated?

2. How the doctrine of the covenant of works was formulated

How did the older covenant theologians go from the garden to the covenant of works? The answer is that they utilized long-acknowledged hermeneutical principles somewhat typical of the entire Christian theological tradition from the early centuries to the post-Reformation era.[2] In other words, they utilized a pre-critical or pre-Enlightenment method of interpreting Scripture. They believed the Bible was not to be interpreted like any other book. They believed the Bible was the written Word of God and that it was its only infallible interpreter. They not only believed the writers of Scripture to be God's penmen, they also saw them to be infallible theologians as they wrote, due to the

---

[2] A good case can be made that the principles they used predate post-apostolic reflection and are imbedded in the text of Scripture (Old and New Testament) itself. Proving this is beyond the scope of this book.

doctrine of the divine inspiration of Holy Scripture. They believed that the Bible often interpreted itself and that later texts often used earlier texts in a way that gave the divine, and therefore infallible because inspired, interpretation of those earlier texts.

The Importance of Hermeneutics in Theological Formulation

In the 1980s, one of my seminary professors said something like this: "The differences between covenant theology and Dispensationalism are, at bottom, hermeneutical differences." I think he was right. I also think that the differences between much of what New Covenant Theology (NCT) advocates and a covenantal Baptist (i.e., 2LCF) perspective are, at bottom, hermeneutical ones. We read the same texts through different interpretive lenses. In a conversation several years ago with Dr. Vern Poythress, I asked him, "Dr. Poythress, is it true that if you get the garden wrong you get eschatology wrong?" Dr. Poythress responded, "If you get the garden wrong, you will get everything wrong." Though there is probably hyperbole in Dr. Poythress' answer, he is essentially correct.

Dispensationalism and NCT get major aspects of the Bible's teaching on the covenant of works wrong because they get the garden wrong, and they get the garden wrong because they get crucial aspects of hermeneutics wrong. This ends up affecting their systems adversely (though there is movement in a better direction by some NCT writers). I will argue, among other things, that a proper hermeneutic leads to affirming the covenant of works in the garden of Eden.

Understanding the Bible's teaching on covenants is crucial. Echoing this sentiment, C. H. Spurgeon says:

> The doctrine of the covenant lies at the root of all true theology. It has been said that he who well understands the distinction between the covenant of works and the covenant of grace, is a master of divinity. I am persuaded that most of the mistakes which men make concerning the doctrines of Scripture are based upon fundamental errors with regard to the covenants of law and grace.[3]

---

[3] This comes from C. H. Spurgeon, "Sermon XL, the Covenant," *The Sermons of Rev. C. H. Spurgeon of London,* 9th Series (New York: Robert Cater & Brothers, 1883), 172, as quoted in Pascal Denault, *The Distinctiveness of Baptist*

The seventeenth-century Particular Baptist Nehemiah Coxe, while discussing God's transactions with Adam, says:

> If a man misses the right account of this, he is certainly bewildered in all further searching for that truth which most concerns him to know.[4]

I agree with these men about the importance of getting the covenant theology of the Bible right.

It will be helpful to remind ourselves of some hermeneutical principles utilized by those who formulated the 2LCF, the Westminster Standards (its Confession [WCF] and Catechisms), and Savoy Declaration (SD). As will be explained below, on the issue of the covenant works, I think these old documents got it right (though the 2LCF differs with the WCF and SD at points which will be discussed below). The hermeneutical principles utilized

---

Covenant Theology: A Comparison Between Seventeenth-Century Particular Baptist and Paedobaptist Federalism (Birmingham, AL: Solid Ground Christian Books, 2013), 6, n. 4.

[4] Nehemiah Coxe and John Owen, *Covenant Theology: From Adam to Christ*, ed. Ronald D. Miller, James M. Renihan, and Francisco Orozco (Palmdale, CA: Reformed Baptist Academic Press, 2005), 42.

Doctrinal Formulation and Hermeneutics

by the men who wrote those creedal documents pre-date the Westminster Assembly, going all the way back to the canonical writers of the Hebrew Scriptures, though space does not permit me to prove such. In the history of Christian thought, these principles are what we might label as pre-critical or pre-Enlightenment.[5] They were utilized by the catholic theological tradition from the early centuries of Christian reflection upon Scripture through the post-Reformation era. In that sense, they are not exclusively Reformed or Protestant. It is of interest to note that these pre-critical hermeneutical principles were the interpretive foundations from which the great creeds, confessions, and catechisms of the church were formed. Four principles are worthy of noting at this time. Space will not allow me to illustrate all of these from the Scriptures in the brief discussion below, though they (and others) will be illustrated throughout this book where I seek to give scriptural

---

[5] See David C. Steinmetz, "The Superiority of Pre-Critical Exegesis," *Theology Today* (April 1980): 27-38, for an introduction to pre-critical hermeneutics. See also Moisés Silva, "Has the Church Misread the Bible?," in *Foundations of Contemporary Interpretation*, gen. ed. Moisés Silva (Grand Rapids: Zondervan Publishing House, 1996).

explication of the doctrinal formulation of the covenant of works found in the 2LCF.

1. The Holy Spirit is the only infallible interpreter of Holy Scripture.[6]

As an example of this principle, John Owen says:

> The only unique, public, authentic, and infallible interpreter of Scripture is none other than the Author of Scripture Himself . . . that is, God the Holy Spirit.[7]

Nehemiah Coxe says, ". . . the best interpreter of the Old Testament is the Holy Spirit speaking to us in the new."[8] This meant that they saw the Bible's interpretation and use of itself as infallible and with interpretive principles embedded in it. When the Bible

---

[6] The material under the next four sub-headings is taken (with permission and slight modification) from Richard C. Barcellos, "Getting the Garden Right: From Hermeneutics to the Covenant of Works," in *By Common Confession: Essays in Honor of James M. Renihan*, ed. Ronald S. Baines, Richard C. Barcellos, and James P. Butler (Palmdale, CA: RBAP, 2015), 201-05.

[7] John Owen, *Biblical Theology or The Nature, Origin, Development, and Study of Theological Truth in Six Books* (Pittsburgh, PA: Soli Deo Gloria Publications, 1994), 797.

[8] Coxe and Owen, *Covenant Theology*, 36.

comments upon, or utilizes itself in any fashion (e.g., direct quotation, allusion, echo, or fulfillment in the OT or NT), it is God's interpretation and, therefore, the divine understanding of how texts should be understood by men. This often means that later texts shed interpretive light on earlier texts. This occurs not only when the New Testament uses the Old Testament, but it occurs in the Old Testament itself, which will be illustrated in our discussion below. Or, we could put it this way: subsequent revelation often makes explicit what is implicit in antecedent revelation.[9] This principle led the older theologians to three more related concepts.

2. The Analogy of Scripture (*Analogia Scriptura*)

Here is Richard A. Muller's definition of *analogia Scripturae*:

the interpretation of unclear, difficult, or ambiguous passages of Scripture by

---

[9] See Vern S. Poythress, "Biblical Hermeneutics," in *Seeing Christ in all of Scripture: Hermeneutics at Westminster Theological Seminary*, ed. Peter A. Lillback (Philadelphia, PA: Westminster Seminary Press, 2016), 14, where he says: "The later communications build on the earlier. What is implicit in the earlier often becomes explicit in the later."

comparison with clear and unambiguous passages *that refer to the same teaching or event.*[10]

An example of this would be utilizing a passage in Matthew to help understand a passage dealing with the same subject in Mark. This principle, as with the first one, obviously presupposes the divine inspiration of Scripture.

The principle of *analogia Scripturae* gained confessional status as follows: "The infallible rule of interpretation of scripture is the scripture itself . . ." (2LCF 1.9).

3. The Analogy of Faith (*Analogia Fidei*)
Muller defines *analogia fidei* as follows:

the use of a general sense of the meaning of Scripture, constructed from the clear or unambiguous *loci* [i.e., places] . . ., as the basis for interpreting unclear or ambiguous texts. As distinct from the more basic *analogia Scripturae* . . ., the *analogia fidei* presupposes a sense of the theological meaning of Scripture.[11]

---

[10] Richard A. Muller, *Dictionary of Latin and Greek Theological Terms* (Grand Rapids: Baker Book House, 1985, Second printing, September 1986), 33; emphasis added.

[11] Muller, *Dictionary*, 33.

This principle has not always been understood properly. For example, Walter C. Kaiser, Jr. fails to distinguish properly between *analogia Scripturae* and *analogia fidei* and advocates what he calls "The Analogy of (Antecedent) Scripture."[12] While analyzing the principle of the analogy of faith, he says:

> Our problem here is whether the analogy of faith is a hermeneutical tool that is 'open [theological] sesame' for every passage of Scripture.[13]

While discussing his proposal for "The Analogy of (Antecedent) Scripture," Kaiser confidently asserts:

> Surely most interpreters will see the wisdom and good sense in limiting our theological observations to conclusions drawn from the text being exegeted and from texts which preceded it in time.[14]

---

[12] Walter C. Kaiser, Jr., *Toward An Exegetical Theology* (1981; reprint, Grand Rapids: Baker Book House, Sixth printing, January 1987), 134ff.

[13] Kaiser, *Toward An Exegetical Theology*, 135; bracketed word original.

[14] Kaiser, *Toward An Exegetical Theology*, 137.

In the conclusion to his discussion, he says:

> However, in no case must that *later* teaching be used exegetically (or in any other way) to unpack the meaning or to enhance the usability of the individual text which is the object of our study.[15]

This is, at worst, a denial of the historic understanding of *analogia fidei* and, at best, a very unhelpful and dangerous modification of the principle. This would mean, for example, that we cannot utilize anything in the Bible outside of Genesis 1-3 to help us interpret it. Since there is nothing in the Bible antecedent to Genesis 1-3, interpreters are left with no subsequent divine use, no subsequent divine explanation of how to understand those chapters. This method ends up defeating itself when we consider that Genesis (and all other books of the Bible) was never intended to stand on its own.[16] As well, the Bible itself (OT and

---

[15] Kaiser, *Toward An Exegetical Theology*, 140; emphasis original.

[16] The OT is not an end itself; it is heading somewhere and demands answers to various issues left unfulfilled. It sets the stage for God's future acts of redemption and assumes that God will follow his redemptive acts with corresponding redemptive-revelational words. The OT cannot stand on its own; it is an open-ended book and must be interpreted as such. The NT provides the rest of

NT) comments on antecedent texts, helping its

---

the story. See Dennis E. Johnson, *Him We Proclaim: Preaching Christ from All the Scriptures* (Phillipsburg, NJ: P&R Publishing, 2007), 160, n. 51, where he takes Kaiser to task for claiming that the OT can stand on its own. In Walter C. Kaiser, Jr., *Preaching and Teaching from the Old Testament: A Guide for the Church* (Grand Rapids: Baker, 2003), 27, he claims: "The Old Testament can stand on its own, for it has done so both in the pre-Christian and the early Christian centuries." Johnson replies: "As will be argued in Chapter 6, the preacher to the Hebrews saw in the Old Testament Scriptures themselves various indications that the Old Testament and its institutions could not 'stand on their own['] but testified to a better, more 'perfect' order to come." Johnson's book is highly recommended. Reading and interpreting the OT on its own is like reading the Gospels without the Epistles, the Epistles without the Gospels, the Prophets without the Pentateuch, the Pentateuch without the Prophets, and the NT without the OT. Kaiser's position seems to entail reading and interpreting the OT without the New. If this is the case, it would give the appearance of over-emphasizing the human authorial element of Holy Scripture. The apostle Peter informs us, concerning the writing prophets of the OT: "It was revealed to them that they were not serving themselves, but you, in these things which now have been announced to you through those who preached the gospel to you by the Holy Spirit sent from heaven—things into which angels long to look" (1 Pet. 1:12). The prophets wrote with a future-oriented messianic consciousness. What they predicted happened when our Lord came and the NT interprets our Lord in light of the OT.

Doctrinal Formulation and Hermeneutics

readers understand the divine intention of those texts. Kaiser's method seems to imply that the exegesis of a given biblical text is to be conducted as if no subsequent biblical texts exist. We must realize that, in one sense, we have an advantage that the biblical writers did not have—we have a completed canon. But we must also realize that the Bible's use of itself (whenever and however this occurs) is infallible. If this is so, then the exegete, using tools outside of the biblical text under consideration, ought to consult *all* possible useful tools, which includes how the Bible comments upon itself no matter where or how it does so. If the Holy Spirit is the only infallible interpreter of Holy Scripture, then certainly exegetes ought to utilize biblical texts outside of Genesis to aid in the understanding of it. It seems to me that Kaiser's proposal would give warrant for exegetes to consult fallible commentaries on Genesis to aid in its interpretation, but deny the use of the Bible itself (which contains inspired and infallible commentary) to that same end.

An example of the proper understanding and use of the analogy of faith would be identifying the serpent of Genesis 3. We can say with utter certainty that the serpent is the devil and Satan. We know this because God tells us via subsequent Scripture in Revelation 12:9, "And the great dragon was thrown down, the serpent of old who is called the devil and Satan" and 20:2, "And he laid hold of the dragon, the serpent of old, who is the devil and Satan." So, according to the analogy of faith, we can affirm that the serpent of Genesis 3 is the devil and Satan.

The inspired and infallible rule of faith is the whole of Scripture, whose textual parts must be understood in light of its textual-theological whole. This insures that the theological forest is not lost for the individual textual trees. It should keep us from doing theology concordance-style, doing word-studies as an end-all to interpretation, and counting texts that use the same words and drawing theological conclusions from it. These methods often do not consider the meaning of the text (or word) under investigation in light of the various levels of context (i.e., phrase, clause, sentence, pericope, book, author, testament, or canon) in which it occurs. The principle of the analogy of faith also warrants that, when we are seeking to understand any text of Scripture (e.g., Gen. 1-3), all texts of Scripture are fair game in the interpretive process. Or it could be stated this way: *the context of every biblical text is all biblical texts.*

The principle of *analogia fidei* gained confessional status as follows:

> The infallible rule of interpretation of scripture is the scripture itself; and therefore, when there is a question about the true and full sense of any scripture, (which is not manifold, but one,) it must be searched and known by other places that speak more clearly. (2LCF 1.9)

4. The Scope of the Scriptures (*Scopus Scripturae*)

Terms such as Christ-centered and Christocentric are used often in modern parlance. But what do they mean? The older way of naming the concept these terms point to, the target or end to which the entirety of the Bible tends, is encapsulated by the Latin phrase *scopus Scripturae* (i.e., the scope of the Scriptures). This concept gained confessional status in the WCF, the SD, and the 2LCF in 1.5, which, speaking of Holy Scripture, say, ". . . the scope of the whole (which is to give all glory to God) . . ."

Reformation and post-Reformation Reformed theologians understood scope in two senses. It had a narrow sense—i.e., the scope of a given text or passage, its basic thrust—but it also had a wider sense—i.e., the target or bull's eye to which all of Scripture tends.[17] It is to this second sense that we will give our attention.

Scope, in the sense intended here, refers to the center or target of the entire canonical revelation; it is that to which the entire Bible points. And whatever that is, it must condition our interpretation of any and every part of Scripture. For the federal or covenant theologians of the seventeenth century, the scope of Scripture was the glory of God in the redemptive work of the incarnate Son of God.[18]

---

17 See the discussion in Richard A. Muller, *Post-Reformation Reformed Dogmatics: The Rise and Development of Reformed Orthodoxy, ca. 1520 to ca. 1725, Volume Two – Holy Scripture* (Grand Rapids: Baker Academic, 2003 [Second Edition]), 206-23, where he discusses these distinctions. See also James M. Renihan, "Theology on Target: The Scope of the Whole (which is to give all glory to God)," *RBTR* II:2 (July 2005): 36-52; Richard C. Barcellos, "*Scopus Scripturae*: John Owen, Nehemiah Coxe, our Lord Jesus Christ, and a Few Early Disciples on Christ as the Scope of Scripture," *Journal of the Institute of Reformed Baptist Studies* [*JIRBS*] (2015): 5-24; and Stephen J. Casselli, *Divine Rule Maintained: Anthony Burgess, Covenant Theology, and the Place of the Law in Reformed Scholasticism* (Grand Rapids: Reformation Heritage Books, 2016), 102-07.

18 See my forthcoming *The Doxological Trajectory of Scripture: God Getting Glory for Himself through what He does*

Their view of the scope of Scripture was itself a conclusion from Scripture, not a presupposition brought to it, and it conditioned all subsequent interpretation.

William Ames, for example, asserts:

> The Old and New Testaments are reducible to these two primary heads. The Old promises Christ to come and the New testifies that he has come.[19]

Likewise, John Owen says, "Christ is . . . the principal end of the whole of Scripture . . ."[20] He continues elsewhere:

> This principle is always to be retained in our minds in reading of the Scripture, — namely, that the revelation and doctrine of the person of Christ and his office, is the foundation whereon all other instructions of the prophets and apostles for the edification

---

in His Son — *An Exegetical and Theological Case Study*, Chapter 5, "Christ as *Scopus Scripturae* — John Owen and Nehemiah Coxe on Christ as the Scope of Scripture for the Glory of God."

[19] William Ames, *The Marrow of Theology* (Durham, NC: The Labyrinth Press, 1983), 1.38.5 (202).

[20] John Owen, *The Works of John Owen*, 23 vols., ed. William H. Goold (Edinburgh: The Banner of Truth Trust, 1987 edition), 1:74.

of the church are built, and whereunto they are resolved . . . So our Lord Jesus Christ himself at large makes it manifest, Luke xxiv. 26, 27, 45, 46. Lay aside the consideration hereof, and the Scriptures are no such thing as they pretend unto, — namely, a revelation of the glory of God in the salvation of the church . . .[21]

Coxe says, ". . . in all our search after the mind of God in the Holy Scriptures we are to manage our inquiries with reference to Christ."[22]

Their Christocentric interpretation of the Bible was a principle derived from the Bible itself, and an application of *sola Scriptura* to the issue of hermeneutics. In other words, they viewed the Bible's authority as extending to how we interpret the Bible. Or it could be stated this way: they saw the authority of Scripture extending to the interpretation of Scripture.[23] These hermeneutical principles (and others) will be utilized throughout chapter 4 of this book.

---

[21] Owen, *Works*, 1:314-15.

[22] Coxe and Owen, *Covenant Theology*, 33.

[23] See Poythress, "Biblical Hermeneutics," 11, where he says: "We use the Bible to derive hermeneutical principles. Then we use hermeneutics to interpret the Bible."

2.

The Doctrine of the
Covenant of Works
in the Confession of Faith

There was a time when I thought that the 2LCF was substantially different from the WCF and SD on the doctrine of the covenant of works. The reasoning was simple. The 2LCF does not say what the other Confessions say about the covenant of works in chapter 7. Both the WCF and the SD assert in 7.2:

> The first covenant made with man was a covenant of works, wherein life was promised to Adam; and in him to his posterity, upon condition of perfect and personal obedience.

The 2LCF does not contain this paragraph (see the text of the 2LCF 7.1-2 below). The conclusion was that the Particular Baptists must have held to a different view of Adam in the garden. I now believe I was wrong. Others hold this view or something similar to it: viz., since 7.2 of the WCF and SD was deleted by the Baptists, their theology of the garden was different. Anyone who holds this view is incorrect for several reasons, which will be discussed below.

At this point, six observations will be offered upon the 2LCF 7.1-2 to aid in understanding what it asserts concerning the covenant of works. These paragraphs were chosen for three reasons: first, the title of chapter 7 is "Of God's Covenant"; second, the language of the 2LCF 7.2 is not the same as the WCF and SD, which has been the cause of some concluding the doctrine of the covenant of works is absent or considerably altered; and third, although the phrase "covenant of works" is absent, the concept is present. We will then move to broader considerations of the 2LCF which will be offered to prove that its formulation, though differing in form (i.e., the way it is stated), is materially (i.e., the substance that is stated) the same as the WCF and SD.

Six Observations upon the 2LCF 7.1-2

Here are the paragraphs which will be examined below followed by six observations:

> The distance between God and the creature is so great, that although reasonable creatures do owe obedience to him as their creator, yet they could never have attained the reward of life but by some voluntary condescension on God's part, which he hath been pleased to express by way of covenant. (2LCF 7.1)

> Moreover, man having brought himself under the curse of the law by his fall, it pleased the Lord to make a covenant of grace, wherein he freely offereth unto sinners life and salvation by Jesus Christ, requiring of them faith in him, that they may be saved; and promising to give unto all those that are ordained unto eternal life, his Holy Spirit, to make them willing and able to believe. (2LCF 7.2)

1. It is important to realize the confessional context of this chapter.

Chapter 7, "Of God's Covenant," comes after the chapter on creation, chapter 4, "Of

Creation," and after the chapter on sin, chapter 6, "Of the Fall of Man, of Sin, and of the Punishment Thereof." Chapter 7 comes before chapter 8, "Of Christ the Mediator."[1] The order is creation, fall, covenant, and then the mediator of salvation.[2]

2. It is important to understand the flow of thought in 7.1-2.

Here is my attempt at an outline of part of 7.1-2.

A. The Absolute Necessity of God's Covenant (2LCF 7.1)
   1. Because of the Creator/creature distinction (2LCF 7.1a); *The distance between God and the creature is so*

---

[1] See the helpful outline of the 2LCF in James M. Renihan, "Covenant Theology in the First and Second London Confessions of Faith" in *Recovering a Covenantal Heritage: Essays in Baptist Covenant Theology*, ed. Richard C. Barcellos (Palmdale, CA: RBAP, 2014), 61-62.

[2] I noted the order to show the progressive development of doctrinal formulation in the Confession. The later chapters assume the former and the former prepare for the later. This means that chapter 7 assumes the chapters prior to it and the doctrinal assertions therein. As will be argued below, the 2LCF 7.1-2 does not use the phrase "covenant of works" for at least two reasons: first, it is assumed from 2LCF 4 and 6 and second, 2LCF 7 concentrates primarily upon the covenant of grace, especially paragraphs 2 and 3.

great, that although reasonable creatures do owe obedience to him as their creator

2. Because the reward of life could never be attained apart from the condescension of God (2LCF 7.1b); *yet they could never have attained the reward of life but by some voluntary condescension on God's part, which he hath been pleased to express by way of covenant*

B. The Essential Characteristics of God's Covenant (2LCF 7.2)

1. Its Subsequent Necessity (2LCF 7.2a); *Moreover, man having brought himself under the curse of the law by his fall*

2. Its Divine Basis (2LCF 7.2b); *it pleased the Lord*

3. Its Gracious Nature (2LCF 7.2c); *to make a covenant of grace*

4. Its Specific Elements (2LCF 7.2d, e); *wherein . . .*

Notice that the necessity of God's covenant with man is grounded in two realities. The first is the Creator/creature distinction ("The distance between God and the creature is so great, that although reasonable creatures do owe obedience to him as their creator"). The second is the necessity of condescension on

God's part for the attaining of "the reward of life" ("yet they could never have attained the reward of life but by some voluntary condescension on God's part, which he hath been pleased to express by way of covenant"). Reasonable creatures owe God obedience (2LCF 4.2-3), but the reward of life is added or promised "by some voluntary condescension on God's part." This "voluntary condescension" God "hath been pleased to express by way of covenant."

3. It is important to understand how 7.2 relates to 7.1.

Notice the word "Moreover" in paragraph 2. This means something like in addition to what has been said, further, or besides. It is an expansion on what has been said in light of Adam's fall into sin (2LCF 6.1). The implication is that God voluntarily condescended "by way of covenant" for the attaining of "the reward of life" (see 2LCF 7.1 and 6.1, ". . . gave him a righteous law, which had been unto life had he kept it . . ."), but man fell in Adam and was brought "under the curse of the law by his fall," thus necessitating "a covenant of grace." The "curse of the law" in 7.2 refers to the threatened death of Genesis 2:16-17.

4. Notice to what the following words refer: "The distance between God and the creature is so great, that although reasonable creatures [see 2LCF 4.2] do owe obedience to him as their creator" (2LCF 7.1a).

These words refer to what man as creature owes to God as Creator.[3] Here the Creator/creature distinction is expressed. Reasonable creatures owe obedience to God because he is their Creator, specifically due to the constitution of man as made in the image of God.

5. Notice the words "yet they could never have attained the reward of life but by some voluntary condescension on God's part" (2LCF 7.1b).

The clause means that "the reward of life" is not based exclusively on the Creator/creature relationship stated in 7.1a. This becomes clear by the next observation and explanation.

---

[3] See the discussions by Robert Shaw, *An Exposition of the Westminster Confession of Faith* (Fearn Ross-shire, Scotland: Christian Focus Publications, 1998), 123 and A. A. Hodge, *The Confession of Faith* (1869; reprint, Edinburgh; Carlisle, PA: The Banner of Truth Trust, 1983), 120-21.

The Doctrine of the Covenant of Works in the 2LCF

6. Notice that the words "which he hath been pleased to express by way of covenant" tell us what God's "voluntary condescension" is.

The clause "which he hath been pleased to express by way of covenant" tells us to what God's "voluntary condescension" refers, which contains the promise of "the reward of life." This principle of "the reward of life" related to "some voluntary condescension on God's part" implies a covenantal revelation of such, though not absolutely coeval or contemporary with Adam's created status. This is what has been termed "the covenant of works."

Though man as a reasonable or rational creature owes God obedience because created,[4] "the reward of life" for obedience is a covenantal stipulation, not a strictly or absolutely creational one. In other words, there were two pre-fall states in which Adam existed—as a reasonable creature of God, owing obedience to his Creator, and as a reasonable creature of God in covenant with

---

[4] The 2LCF 7.1 cites Luke 17:10, which says, "So you too, when you do all the things which are commanded you, say, 'We are unworthy slaves; we have done *only* that which we ought to have done.'" Man owes God obedience because he is a reasonable or rational creature of God.

him, owing obedience to his covenantal Lord.[5] A. A. Hodge, commenting on WCF 7.1 says:

> The very act of creation brings the creature under obligation to the Creator, but it cannot bring the Creator into obligation to the creature.[6]

Robert Shaw, commenting on the same text states, "God entered into a covenant with Adam in his state of innocence."[7] This seems to imply that Adam existed in a state of innocence and, while existing in that state, God entered into a covenant with him. Is this what is intended by the WCF, SD, and 2LCF? It will help at this juncture to explore this a bit further.

Where did God enter into a covenant with Adam?[8] Consider the fact that man was made

---

[5] See the discussions in Rowland S. Ward, *God & Adam: Reformed Theology and the Creation Covenant* (Wantirna, Australia: New Melbourne Press, 2003), 59-66 and 99-103. Ward uses the language "two pre-fall states" on p. 61 (see also 99ff.). Casselli, *Divine Rule Maintained*, 69ff. points out the careful distinctions made by the seventeenth-century Reformed theologians on this issue.

[6] Hodge, *Confession of Faith*, 121.

[7] Shaw, *Exposition*, 124.

[8] This question obviously assumes that God entered into covenant with Adam for the sake of the discussion about the Confession.

then the garden was made into which he was placed. Genesis 2:7-8 says:

> Then the LORD God formed man of dust from the ground, and breathed into his nostrils the breath of life; and man became a living being. 8 The LORD God planted a garden toward the east, in Eden; and there He placed the man whom He had formed.

Genesis 2:15 says, "Then the LORD God took the man and put him into the garden of Eden to cultivate it and keep it." Man was created then placed in the garden. Man's vocation was not absolutely coeval with his creation. This distinction between man as creature of God and man in covenant with God in the garden seems to be what the WCF, SD, and 2LCF teach. The Westminster Larger Catechism (WLC), Q. 20 says:

> Q. 20. *What was the providence of God toward man in the estate in which he was created?*
> A. The providence of God toward man in the estate in which he was created, was *the placing him in paradise*, appointing him to dress it, giving him liberty to eat of the fruit of earth; putting the creatures under his dominion, and ordaining marriage for his

help; affording him communion with
himself; instituting the Sabbath; *entering into
a covenant of life with him*, upon condition of
personal, perfect, and perpetual obedience,
of which the tree of life was a pledge; and
forbidding to eat of the tree of the
knowledge of good and evil, upon the pain
of death. (emphasis added)

Notice that the WLC discusses the covenant of
works under the doctrine of divine providence,
which begins at Q. 18. ("What are God's works
of providence?") and comes after the questions
dealing with creation (i.e., questions 15-17). The
Westminster Shorter Catechism (WSC) and the
Baptist Catechism (BC) do the same thing. In
the estate in which man was created, God
revealed to him what is termed "a covenant of
life," which is a synonym for the covenant of
works, after "placing him in paradise." The
covenant of works, then, is not absolutely
coeval with the act of man's creation.[9] Man was

---

[9] See Barcellos, *The Family Tree*, 164-66, under the
heading "EXCURSUS: The Temporal Revelation of the
Covenant of Works in Owen — Absolutely or Relatively
Coeval with Creation?" and Ward, *God & Adam*, chapter 4,
entitled "Emergence of a post-creation, pre-fall covenant,"
59-66 and chapter 11 entitled "Law and covenant: the two
states of the pre-fall Adam," 99-103.

The Doctrine of the Covenant of Works in the 2LCF

created *for* covenant, but strictly speaking not *in* the covenant of works.[10] The creation of man and man in the covenant of works with God can be distinguished but they should not be separated.[11] The *matter* of the covenant of works, the law written on Adam's heart due to man being created in the image of God, is present at his creation, however, the *form* of the covenant of works was revealed to him by God as found in (at least) Genesis 2:16-17.[12] Though

---

[10] Thanks to Samuel Renihan for first mentioning this formulation to me. See Joel R. Beeke & Mark Jones, *A Puritan Theology: Doctrine for Life* (Grand Rapids: Reformation Heritage Books, 2012), 223-24, under the heading, "Made *In* or *For* a Covenant?" The 2LCF hints at this distinction in these words: "After God had made all other creatures, he created man, male and female, with reasonable and immortal souls, rendering them fit *unto* [emphasis added] that life to God *for which* [emphasis added] they were created . . ." (2LCF 4.2a). Man was created "fit unto that life for which they were created . . ." This seems to imply the distinction for which I am arguing. Whether that is the case or not, in chapter 4 it will become clear that many seventeenth-century (and subsequent) Reformed theologians viewed the covenant of works as offering a quality of life not endowed upon man at his creation.

[11] See Ward, *God & Adam*, 99.

[12] According to Ward, this is the view found in Edward Fisher's *The Marrow of Modern Divinity*. See Ward,

beyond the scope of this chapter's discussion, it is important to realize that the Confession asserts that man, male and female, was

> made after the image of God, in knowledge, righteousness, and true holiness [citing Eccles. 7:29 and Gen. 1:26]; having the law of God written in their hearts [citing Rom. 2:14-15] . . . (2LCF 4.2).

Adam's responsibility to obey God is based on creation; once put in the garden, however, a positive[13] aspect of his obedience is added by the words of Genesis 2:16-17. This is reflected in 2LCF 6.1 and 19.1.

> Although God created man upright and perfect, and gave him a righteous law, which had been unto life had he kept it, and threatened death upon the breach thereof [citing Gen. 2:16-17], yet he did not long abide in this honour; Satan using the subtlety of the serpent to subdue Eve, then

---

God & Adam, 102. Thanks to Dabney Olguin for stimulating discussions on this issue.

[13] "Positive" refers to that which is in addition to nature or creation. The law written on the heart of man at creation and the obedience owed the Creator is natural; the positive law, being in addition to nature, brings man formally into covenant with his Creator.

by her seducing Adam, who, without any compulsion, did willfully transgress the law of their creation, and the command given unto them, in eating the forbidden fruit, which God was pleased, according to his wise and holy counsel to permit, having purposed to order it to his own glory. (2LCF 6.1)

God gave to Adam a law of universal obedience written in his heart [echoing 2LCF 4.2, quoted above], and a particular precept of not eating the fruit of the tree of knowledge of good and evil [echoing 2LCF 6.1]; by which he bound him and all his posterity to personal, entire, exact, and perpetual obedience; promised life upon the fulfilling, and threatened death upon the breach of it, and endued him with power and ability to keep it. (2LCF 19.1)

As stated above, Adam's created state and covenantal state unto life may be distinguished but ought not to be separated. This distinction is reflected in the WCF, SD, 2LCF, WLC, WSC, BC, and in many writers of that era.[14]

---

[14] Another way the distinction was maintained has to do with the concept of man's restipulation. For example, Coxe says: ". . . a covenant relationship to God and interest in him does not immediately result from the

Man's obedience is naturally necessary due to being God's creature in his image. Anything above this, such as "the reward of life," comes from God's "voluntary condescension . . ., which he hath been pleased to express by way of covenant" (2LCF 7.1). Casselli, commenting on the view of Westminster Assembly member Anthony Burgess, says:

> Adam by virtue of creation owes perfect obedience to God, which obedience strictly

---

proposal of a covenant and terms of a covenant relationship to man. But it is by restipulation that man actually enters into covenant with God and becomes an interested party in the covenant. It is a mutual consent of the parties in covenant that states [To instate or establish in covenant.] and completes a covenant relationship." See Coxe and Owen, *Covenant Theology*, 35. The bracketed words are an editorial footnote in the Coxe and Owen book. The concept of restipulation, according to some, does not apply universally or to all biblical covenants. For example, the Noahic covenant is a covenant of unconditional promise. No one had to do any work of the law or believe in the gospel for the promise of that covenant to be fulfilled. The concept of restipulation is also termed dipleuric. For discussion on the terms monopleuric and dipleuric in the context of covenantal revelations of God to man see Barcellos, *The Family Tree*, 91, 97, 98, 101, 163, 164, 165, 187, and 204, and the sources cited there. For definitions of these terms see Muller, *Dictionary*, 120 and 122.

merits nothing from God, but which God graciously chooses to reward on the basis of the covenant established by Him.[15]

Coxe says that God added to the law written on Adam's heart a positive law in the garden of Eden. Recall that man was placed in the garden after he was created. Here are Coxe's own words:

> It pleased the Sovereign Majesty of Heaven to add to this eternal law [i.e., the internal law written on man's heart via the creative act of God] a positive precept in which he charged man not to eat of the fruit of one tree in the midst of the garden of Eden.[16]

Coxe also says:

> In this lies the mystery of the first transaction of God with man and of his relationship to God founded on it. *This did not result immediately from the law of his creation but from the disposition of a covenant according to the free, sovereign, and wise counsel of God's will.* Therefore, although the law of creation is easily understood by men (and

---

15 Casselli, *Divine Rule Maintained*, 72.
16 Coxe and Owen, *Covenant Theology*, 43.

there is little controversy about it among those that are not degenerate from all principles of reason and humanity), yet the covenant of creation, the interest of Adam's posterity with him in it, and the guilt of original sin returning on them by it, are not owned by the majority of mankind. Nor can they be understood except by the light of divine revelation.[17]

It is not from any necessity of nature that God enters into covenant with men but of his own good pleasure. Such a privilege and nearness to God as is included in covenant interest *cannot immediately result from the relationship which they have to God as reasonable creatures,* though upright and in a perfect state.[18]

The "voluntary condescension" of God was an act of his kind providence, not formally included in the initial act of man's creation. The promise of "the reward of life" is in addition to man's created status. The type of life to be rewarded was not what Adam possessed via creation but what he failed to attain via

---

[17] Coxe and Owen, *Covenant Theology*, 49; emphasis added.

[18] Coxe and Owen, *Covenant Theology*, 36; emphasis added.

covenant or, as the WCF says, the "fruition of [God] as their blessedness and reward" (WCF 7.1). It is this quality of life that our Lord Jesus merited by his covenantal obedience as the last Adam which he brings to and confers upon all gospel-believing sinners. This is termed the covenant of grace and is the focus of chapter 7 of the 2LCF.

Though chapter 7 of the 2LCF does not use the phrase "covenant of works," the doctrinal concept of it is clearly implied in all three paragraphs (see below for brief discussion of the 2LCF 7.3). It is also implied in 4.3, 6.1, chapter 8, and 19.1 as well. The phrase is used explicitly in 19.6 (2x) and 20.1.

Reasons why the 2LCF Contains the Same Doctrine of the Covenant of Works as the WCF and SD

Taking a wider look at the 2LCF in order to see the doctrinal assertions, the assumptions of earlier formulations within the document, and the explicit terminology used at various places will bring with it the conclusion that its basic doctrine of the covenant of works comports with the WCF and SD. Six reasons for this claim are offered below.

1. Because the explicit language "covenant of works" occurs in the Confession (19.6 [2x] and 20.1).

Although true believers be not under the law as a *covenant of works*, to be thereby justified or condemned, yet it is of great use to them as well as to others, in that as a rule of life, informing them of the will of God and their duty, it directs and binds them to walk accordingly; discovering also the sinful pollutions of their natures, hearts, and lives, so as examining themselves thereby, they may come to further conviction of, humiliation for, and hatred against, sin; together with a clearer sight of the need they have of Christ and the perfection of his obedience; it is likewise of use to the regenerate to restrain their corruptions, in that it forbids sin; and the threatenings of it serve to shew what even their sins deserve, and what afflictions in this life they may expect for them, although freed from the curse and unallayed rigour thereof. The promises of it likewise shew them God's approbation of obedience, and what blessings they may expect upon the performance thereof, though not as due to them by the law as a *covenant of works*; so as man's doing good and refraining from evil, because the law encourageth to the one and deterreth from the other, is no evidence of his being under the law and not under grace. (2LCF 19.6; emphasis added)

The *covenant of works* being broken by sin, and made unprofitable unto life, God was pleased to give forth the promise of Christ, the seed of the woman, as the means of calling the elect, and begetting in them faith and repentance; in this promise the gospel, as to the substance of it, was revealed, and [is] therein effectual for the conversion and salvation of sinners. (2LCF 20.1; emphasis added)

There is no reason from the Confession or the writings of Nehemiah Coxe, a likely co-editor (senior editor?) of the Confession, or any other Particular Baptist connected to the Confession (as far as I am aware) to think they meant anything other than what their Presbyterian and Congregational brothers meant by the phrase covenant of works. Pascal Denault, supporting this claim, says, "The writings of the [seventeenth-century Particular] Baptists show that they shared this same conception of the Covenant of Works as their paedobaptist

contemporaries."[19] Also, in the Preface to the
Confession, entitled, *"To the Judicious and
Impartial Reader,"* we are assured that the
authors of the Confession used

> the very same words with them both [i.e.,
> Presbyterians and Congregationalists] in
> these articles (which are many) wherein our
> faith and doctrine are the same with theirs;
> and this we did the more abundantly to
> manifest our consent with both in all the
> fundamental articles of the Christian
> religion . . . And also to convince all that we
> have no itch to clog religion with new words
> . . . (xiii)

It is likely this applies to, among other things,
the phrase and doctrine of the covenant of
works. There is no evidence in the primary
document, or any secondary documents of
which I am aware, that they meant anything
different from what others in their day meant
by the phrase covenant of works.

---

[19] Denault, *The Distinctiveness of Baptist Covenant
Theology*, 29. See Renihan, "Covenant Theology in the First
and Second London Confessions of Faith," 45-70.

The Doctrine of the Covenant of Works in the 2LCF

2. Because the doctrine of the covenant of works is contained or implied without the phrase covenant of works in at least five places in the Confession.

First, 2LCF 6.1 says:

> Although God created man upright and perfect, and gave him a righteous law, which had been unto life had he kept it, and threatened death upon the breach thereof, yet he did not long abide in this honour; Satan using the subtlety of the serpent to subdue Eve, then by her seducing Adam, who, without any compulsion, did willfully transgress the law of their creation, and the command given unto them, in eating the forbidden fruit, which God was pleased, according to his wise and holy counsel to permit, having purposed to order it to his own glory.

This is the doctrine of the covenant of works without the phrase. Notice the context in which it occurs—the fall into sin. If we lived in the seventeenth century, we would immediately think "covenant of works" while reading 6.1.

Second, 2LCF 7.1 says:

> The distance between God and the creature is so great, that although reasonable

creatures do owe obedience to him as their creator, yet they could never have attained the reward of life but by some voluntary condescension on God's part, which he hath been pleased to express by way of covenant.

This implies "the reward of life" (not a gift at Adam's creation but a quality of life to be attained via covenant) spoken of in 2LCF 6.1 came by God's "voluntary condescension . . . by way of covenant."

Third, 2LCF 7.2a says, "Moreover, man having brought himself under the curse of the law by his fall." As noted above, "Moreover" should be taken to mean something like in addition to what has been said, further, or besides. It is an expansion on what has already been said in light of Adam's fall into sin. What had already been said? Both 2LCF 7.1 and 2LCF 6.1. The implication is that God voluntarily condescended by way of covenant for the attaining of the reward of life but man fell in Adam and was brought under the curse of the law.

Fourth, 2LCF 7.3b says:

man being now utterly incapable of acceptance with God upon those terms on which Adam stood in his state of innocency.

The Doctrine of the Covenant of Works in the 2LCF

The necessity of the covenant of grace is predicated upon the fact that man is incapable of acceptance with God upon the terms Adam stood upon in his state of innocency (see 2LCF 6.1), and according to 2LCF 7.1, those terms included God's "voluntary condescension . . . by way of covenant."

Fifth, 2LCF 19.1 says:

> God gave to Adam a law of universal obedience written in his heart, and a particular precept of not eating the fruit of the tree of knowledge of good and evil; by which he bound him and all his posterity to personal, entire, exact, and perpetual obedience; promised life upon the fulfilling, and threatened death upon the breach of it, and endued him with power and ability to keep it.

This is the doctrine of the covenant of works without the phrase.

3. Because of the title and emphasis of chapter 7.[20]

Notice the slightly shortened form of this title as compared with the WCF and SD, which

---

[20] Dr. James M. Renihan is to be credited with reasons 3 and 4 (and much more).

read, "Of God's Covenant with Man." The Baptist's title is "Of God's Covenant," which gives the appearance of concentrating on one covenant. This is exactly what happens in 2LCF 7. It concentrates on the covenant of grace and either assumes or implies the covenant of works, making its explicit mention superfluous.

4. Because of the order of the chapters and the shift that takes place at chapter 7.

Chapter 6 is about the fall into sin and its consequences. Chapter 7 introduces us to the covenantal framework of salvation — the covenant of grace. Chapter 8 introduces us to the covenant servant of salvation. Chapters 8-20 cover both the accomplishment (via the covenant of redemption, 2LCF 8.1) and application of redemption. The point is that chapter 7 is foundational and forward-looking.[21] It assumes the broken covenant of works and introduces us to God's remedy — "a

---

[21] See Renihan, "Covenant Theology in the First and Second London Confessions of Faith," 66, where he says: "Its [2LCF 7] paragraph 3 is a wonderful redemptive-historical overview of the covenantal purpose of God in the gospel." He goes on to discuss "the emphasis on the forward movement of redemptive history . . ." reflected in 7.3. He also discusses the forward-looking motif of the covenant theology of the 2LCF in his conclusion (69).

covenant of grace," wherein all its benefits are procured or earned by the incarnate Son of God and conferred upon believing sinners apart from their own works.

5. Because Nehemiah Coxe clearly taught the doctrine of the covenant of works.

In his *A Discourse of the Covenants that God made with men before the law . . .*, Coxe utilized the same terms, phrases, concepts and sources as his paedobaptist brothers. His treatise is

> structured after the federal model, utilizes Reformed orthodox theological nomenclature, concepts, and sources, and is semantically Reformed orthodox . . .[22]

Like others in his day, he called it the covenant of creation,[23] covenant of works,[24] covenant of friendship,[25] and a covenant of rich bounty and goodness.[26]

---

[22] Barcellos, *The Family Tree*, 94. See Coxe and Owen, *Covenant Theology*, 71-140.

[23] Coxe and Owen, *Covenant Theology*, 39, 46, 49, 53, 58.

[24] Coxe and Owen, *Covenant Theology*, 45, 49, 53.

[25] Coxe and Owen, *Covenant Theology*, 49, 51. This seems to be dependent upon Cocceius.

[26] Coxe and Owen, *Covenant Theology*, 49.

6. Because (as far as I am aware) no Particular Baptist of the seventeenth century connected to the Confession denied the covenant of works or thought it needed recasting.

The extant evidence, in fact, is clearly to the contrary. If there is no evidence from the literature of the Particular Baptists of that day that they thought differently about the covenant of works and there is evidence that they agreed with the basic tenets of the doctrine, saying they denied it or thought it needed recasting contradicts what they said. Not only that, it displays a poor method of interpreting documents of antiquity, imposing one's scruples upon an old document and interpreting it in light of those scruples. This is anachronistic, a very poor method of historical interpretation.

Conclusion

Though it could be argued the changes in the 2LCF were both intentional and theologically strategic, this does not necessarily imply these changes were an attempt to alter the doctrine of the covenant of works, or to distance the Particular Baptists from the theology of the covenant of works as found in either the WCF or SD, nor was it to satisfy the scruples of fellow Particular Baptists. There were no such scruples concerning the doctrine of the covenant of works to satisfy.

Now that we have examined the 2LCF on the covenant of works, the next chapter will address a typical objection to the covenant of works and offer a working definition for it.

3.

A Typical Objection to the Covenant of Works and A Working Definition

Before offering some scriptural arguments in favor of the covenant of works, it may help to interact with a typical objection to this doctrine as well as mentioning our working definition of the covenant of works along with some brief discussion.

A Typical Objection to the Covenant of Works

Many have denied the covenant of works for various reasons. For the sake of space, one typical objection will be addressed.

1. The objection stated

Probably the most obvious objection, and a very common one, is that the word "covenant" is nowhere to be found in the first two chapters of Genesis. In fact, the Hebrew word for covenant, *berith*, does not occur in the book of Genesis until chapter 6. These observations lead to the conclusion, so goes the objection, that there is no covenant in the Bible until Genesis 6. A covenant of works in the garden, then, lacks biblical evidence and is, in fact, unbiblical.[1] It is an extra-biblical, human construct imposed on the Bible to justify one's theological system, which obviously needs re-casting. The covenant of works has human origins, not divine origins, so it is claimed. It is man's theology, not God's. Put in the form of a question, this objection can be stated as follows: How can there be a covenant in Genesis 2 if Moses does not say so? My short answer to this legitimate question would be because God says so. But to be fair to any objectors, this objection will be answered under three points of consideration.

---

[1] See Richard L. Mayhue, "New Covenant Theology and Futuristic Premillennialism," *The Master's Seminary Journal*, 18.2 (Fall 2007): 221 and 225 for this kind of argumentation.

2. The objection answered

First, this objection assumes that if a word is not in a text its concept cannot be there either. This is the word-concept fallacy. The Bible itself sees concepts in texts and then uses words that do not occur in the text being referenced to describe those concepts, something that was noted in chapter 1. For example, consider Acts 2 again. Here Peter references Psalm 16:8-11. Notice what he does in 2:31. Acts 2:22-31 says:

> "Men of Israel, listen to these words: Jesus the Nazarene, a man attested to you by God with miracles and wonders and signs which God performed through Him in your midst, just as you yourselves know— 23 this *Man*, delivered over by the predetermined plan and foreknowledge of God, you nailed to a cross by the hands of godless men and put *Him* to death. 24 "But God raised Him up again, putting an end to the agony of death, since it was impossible for Him to be held in its power. 25 "For David says of Him, 'I SAW THE LORD ALWAYS IN MY PRESENCE; FOR HE IS AT MY RIGHT HAND, SO THAT I WILL NOT BE SHAKEN. 26 'THEREFORE MY HEART WAS GLAD AND MY TONGUE EXULTED; MOREOVER MY FLESH ALSO WILL LIVE IN HOPE; 27 BECAUSE YOU WILL NOT ABANDON MY SOUL TO HADES, NOR ALLOW YOUR HOLY ONE TO

UNDERGO DECAY. [28] 'YOU HAVE MADE KNOWN TO ME THE WAYS OF LIFE; YOU WILL MAKE ME FULL OF GLADNESS WITH YOUR PRESENCE.' [29] "Brethren, I may confidently say to you regarding the patriarch David that he both died and was buried, and his tomb is with us to this day. [30] "And so, because he was a prophet and knew that GOD HAD SWORN TO HIM WITH AN OATH TO SEAT *one* OF HIS DESCENDANTS ON HIS THRONE, [31] he looked ahead and spoke of the resurrection of the Christ, that HE WAS NEITHER ABANDONED TO HADES, NOR DID His flesh SUFFER DECAY.

Peter uses *words* that are not in the Psalm to describe *concepts* from the Psalm. He says that David "looked ahead and spoke of the resurrection of the Christ." The words "resurrection" and "Christ" do not occur in the Psalm. Peter uses these words to describe concepts implicit in the Psalm though not used explicitly by the psalmist. The point is that concepts can be present in texts without the words we normally use to describe them. If I said, "Base hit, home run, strike three, and walk-off single," you would, most likely, reduce those phrases and the concepts indicated by them to a single word — baseball — yet I did not use the word baseball.

A Typical Objection and a Working Definition

Second, there are words used outside of the garden narrative to describe Adam and his Edenic vocation which are not contained in it. For example, in Luke 3:38, Adam is called "the son of God." However, Moses does not call Adam the son of God in Genesis and, in fact, the word "son" first occurs in Genesis 4:17 with reference to Enoch's son. If God tells us Adam was a son of God, it does not matter where he tells us. The case is settled, even if he tells us in Luke 3. Also, Adam did not first become a son of God when Luke penned his Gospel. He was constituted as such long before. The concept of Adam as a son of God, therefore, is implicit in the Genesis narrative, even though the word "son" is nowhere to be found there. How do we know this? God tells us in subsequent written revelation, the only infallible interpretation of Holy Scripture we possess.

In Romans 5:14, Adam is called "a type of Him who was to come." However, Moses does not call Adam a type of Christ in Genesis and, in fact, the word "type" first occurs in the Bible in Romans 5:14. If God tells us Adam was a type of Christ, it does not matter where he tells us. The case is settled, even if he tells us in Romans 5. Also, Adam did not first become a type of Christ when Paul penned Romans. The

A Typical Objection and a Working Definition

concept of Adam as a type of Christ, therefore, is implicit in the Genesis narrative, even though the word "type" is nowhere to be found there. How do we know this? God tells us in subsequent written revelation, the only infallible interpretation of Holy Scripture we possess.

In 1 Corinthians 15:22, Paul says, "For as in Adam all die . . ." However, Moses does not tell us that Adam was the representative of men in the Genesis narrative. The phrase "in Adam" is not in the book of Genesis or anywhere else in the Old Testament. As a matter of fact, the phrase "in Adam" occurs only in 1 Corinthians 15:22. If God tells us "in Adam all die," it does not matter where he tells us. The case is settled, even if he tells us in 1 Corinthians 15. Also, all did not die in Adam when Paul penned 1 Corinthians. The concept of Adam as the representative of man in the garden, therefore, is implicit in the Genesis narrative, even though the words "in Adam" are nowhere to be found there. How do we know this? God tells us in subsequent written revelation, the only infallible interpretation of Holy Scripture we possess.

Third, the Bible itself, looking back upon Adam in the garden, uses the explicit language of covenant. Since this is an important link in the argument for the scriptural doctrine of the covenant of works, we will explore this in the next chapter in some detail. For now, let me draw a conclusion to this typical objection.

I think the objection is cleared, though more counter-arguments could be offered. The account of Genesis 1-3 contains more than meets the eye. It is a narrative, not an exhaustive theological essay drawing out all the implications embedded or assumed in its terms. It is one of those texts that ends up being referenced many times in subsequent written revelation. Other texts assume it and draw out of it what is implied in it. What is implicit in it becomes explicit by the subsequent written Word of God. The biblical writers were theologians after all. They not only quoted (and alluded to) biblical texts, they often articulated the meaning of ancient texts in their own words. As stated above, subsequent revelation often makes explicit what is implicit in antecedent revelation. In other words, the Bible often comments upon and explains itself. And, in the case of Adam in the garden, this is exactly what happens in both the Old and New Testaments.

A Working Definition
of the Covenant of Works

Prior to offering scriptural arguments in favor of the doctrine of the covenant of works, a working definition will be offered in order to establish what must be proved. Consideration will be given to defining divine covenants with men and then a proposed definition of the covenant of works will follow.

1. A brief definition of covenant when it relates to God and man

A divine covenant with man may be defined very briefly as a divinely sanctioned commitment or relationship. In this sense, covenants come from God to man. They are not contracts between equal business partners. They are not up for negotiation. They are imposed by God upon man and, as Coxe says, "[for] the advancing and bettering of his state."[2] The divine covenants are not intended to merely sustain man in the condition he was in prior to those covenants being revealed to him. They are, in some sense, intended for "the advancing and bettering of his state." Think of

---

[2] Coxe and Owen, *Covenant Theology*, 36.

the Noahic covenant. Prior to its revelation as found in Genesis 6-9, the earth was potentially subject to a universal flood due to the justice of God being executed on the earth against the wickedness of man. We know this for certain because that is exactly what happened. The Noahic covenant, which includes man (Noah and his descendants), also involves every living creature (Gen. 9:9-10, 15, 16). It embraces and benefits the earth as well (Gen. 8:22 says, "While the earth remains, Seedtime and harvest, And cold and heat, And summer and winter, And day and night Shall not cease"; see Gen. 9:13, "I set My bow in the cloud, and it shall be for a sign of a covenant between Me *and the earth*" [emphasis added]; see also Jer. 33:20, 25 which alludes to the Noahic covenant, "My covenant for the day and My covenant for the night" [Jer. 33:20][3]). That divine covenants are revealed to man for "the advancing and bettering of his state" can be said of all other divine covenants with man throughout the Bible. Abraham (and his carnal and spiritual seed) was better off for the covenant revealed to

---

[3] See Michael G. Brown and Zach Keele, *Sacred Bond: Covenant Theology Explored* (Grandville, MI: Reformed Fellowship, Inc., 2012), 78-79 for this interpretation of Jer. 33.

A Typical Objection and a Working Definition

him. The Israelites were better off for the covenant revealed to them. It promised them blessings from God they did not have promised to them prior to its promulgation. David and the Israelites were better off for the covenant revealed to them. And believers of all ages are much better off for the revelation of the new covenant in its promissory form in the Old Testament and in its concluded, or its historically ratified, form in the New Testament. Coxe also says this while defining covenants between God and man:

> [They involve a] declaration of his sovereign pleasure concerning *the benefits he will bestow on them*, the communion they will have with him, and the way and means by which this will be enjoyed by them.[4]

Note well that Coxe says covenants are imposed on man by God "[for] the advancing and bettering of his state" and that they concern "the benefits he will bestow on them." Improvement and betterment, in some sense, are built into all covenants that God makes with man, and the covenant of works is no

---

4 Coxe and Owen, *Covenant Theology*, 36; emphasis added.

A Typical Objection and a Working Definition

exception.[5] As we will see below, the improvement that the covenant of works proffered was eschatological in nature, something which Adam failed to attain but that which Christ, the last Adam, attained.

2. The definition of the phrase "covenant of works"

Our working definition of the covenant of works is as follows: that divinely sanctioned commitment or relationship God imposed upon Adam, who was a sinless representative of mankind (or a public person), an image-bearing son of God, conditioned upon his obedience, with a penalty for disobedience, all for the bettering of man's state. Here we have the following: 1) sovereign, divine imposition; 2) representation by Adam (i.e., federal or covenantal headship), a sinless image-bearing son of God; 3) a conditional element (i.e., obedience); 4) a penalty for disobedience (i.e., death); and 5) a promise of reward (i.e., eschatological potential or "betterment"). It is important to keep this definition in mind as we work our way through the discussion below. It is also important to recognize that the covenant

---

[5] I am indebted to Samuel Renihan for helping me state my thoughts more clearly on this issue.

A Typical Objection and a Working Definition

of works was made with a representative, sinless image-bearing son of God. It could only be fulfilled by a representative, sinless image-bearing son of God, since that is who it was made with and since disobedience violates its terms, which happened with Adam and all those he represented. Its curse affects Adam and his progeny, but its promised reward is impossible to attain since man is now in a fallen, sinful condition. In order to fulfill its condition and receive its promised reward, another like Adam is necessary.

4.

The Scriptural Arguments for the Covenant of Works in the Garden

The scriptural arguments in favor of the covenant of works in the garden offered below are not exhaustive. All the reasons that could be and have been marshaled in support of this doctrine are not presented. In large part, the arguments are framed to help illustrate the hermeneutical issues mentioned above. It was stated in previous discussion that Dispensationalism and NCT get the garden wrong because they get hermeneutics wrong. The arguments below are attempts to offer a better way of interpreting the garden. The seven arguments, stated as considerations, are as follows:

- Consider Moses' subsequent and inspired, and therefore infallible, reflection upon the acts of God at creation as recorded for us in Genesis 2:4ff.
- Consider the words of the prophet Isaiah.
- Consider the words of the prophet Hosea.
- Consider why it is denominated the "covenant of works."
- Consider the fact that Adam was "a type of Him who was to come."
- Consider the fact that Adam sinned and fell short of something he did not possess via creation.
- Consider the fact that Christ, upon his resurrection, entered into glory.

These considerations reflect a redemptive-historical method, on the main, which seeks to interpret the events in the garden via subsequent divine commentary in the Bible on those very events. As readers will notice, the considerations quickly become Christological. The reason for this will become obvious as one reads through the discussion. It will become clear that what J. V. Fesko asserts about his book *Last Things First: Unlocking Genesis 1–3 with the Christ of Eschatology* applies to the discussion below. Fesko says:

Many come to the chapters [i.e., Gen. 1-3] thinking they know what occurs therein — creation, man, fall — and they then move along never realizing that they have entered the shadowlands, the land of the types of Christ and his work. This book represents my efforts to explain Genesis 1−3 in the light of Christ and eschatology.[1]

The considerations below are an attempt to do what Fesko did. The arguments which follow are cumulative. Each consideration is to be taken on its own, then in concert with the others.

Consider Moses' Subsequent and Inspired, and therefore Infallible, Reflection upon the Acts of God at Creation as Recorded for us in Genesis 2:4ff.

It is important to understand the relationship between God's acts and the Holy Scripture. In large part, Holy Scripture is the recording, interpretation, and application of God's

---

[1] J. V. Fesko, *Last Things First: Unlocking Genesis 1-3 with the Christ of Eschatology* (Fearn, Ross-shire, Scotland: Mentor Imprint by Christian Focus Publications, 2007), 9.

previous acts. In other words, the Scripture writers don't simply record God's acts; they interpret them and apply them in their own words—i.e., they do theology. For example, our Lord Jesus Christ lived and died before the final divine interpretation of his sufferings and glory were given to us in the form and unique words of the New Testament. Likewise, the creating act of God occurred prior to Moses' writing about it (as did all the events subsequent to creation recorded in the Pentateuch). What's the point? In Genesis 2:4, Moses goes from the term *Elohim* for God to the phrase *Yahweh Elohim*, *Yahweh* being the covenantal name of God (cp. Gen. 1:1, 2, 3, 4, 5, 6, 7, 8, 9, 10, 11, 12, 14, 16, 17, 18, 20, 21, 22, 24, 25, 26, 27, 28, 29, 31; 2:2, 3 w. Gen. 2:4, 5, 7, 8, 9, 15, 16, 18, 19, 21, 22). Many believe that at 2:4 Moses goes from creation in general to the apex of the terrestrial creation, man in God's image, and his covenantal responsibility to God. In other words, Moses goes from the creation of man, male and female, to the Edenic vocation of Adam. The use of *Yahweh* here could indicate a covenantal act of God toward Adam. This suggests that covenant and Adam's Edenic vocation or calling go together. Moses, reflecting upon God's act of creation and its immediate aftermath, uses the covenantal name of God in the context of discussing Adam and his Edenic vocation.[2] For us that might not seem to be an issue worth noting. However, for ancient readers/hearers of this passage, they most likely would have noticed the shift in language, a shift with theological and covenantal implications, whether they recognized it or not.[3]

Before moving to the next consideration, it may help to remind readers what was discussed briefly in chapter 2. It was pointed out that the WCF, SD, 2LCF, and the WLC, WSC, and BC view the covenant of works as formally revealed in the garden. A distinction between man's created state and man in covenant with God was observed to be the teaching of the Confessions and Catechisms.

---

[2] See the discussion on Moses' use of the covenantal name of God in Brown and Keele, *Sacred Bond*, 47-48 and the brief discussion on "the compounding of the two divine names" in John D. Currid, *A Study Commentary on Genesis, Volume 1: Genesis 1:1-25:18* (Darlington, UK: Evangelical Press, 2003), 96-97.

[3] I added "whether they recognized it or not" because the text meant and means what it does irrespective of the understanding of its original recipients. Meaning is not in the eye of the beholder.

The Scriptural Arguments for the Covenant of Works

Man was made then the garden was made into which man was placed (Gen. 2:7-8, 15). In Genesis 1:27, Moses informs us that "God [*Elohim*] created man in His own image, in the image of God He created him; male and female He created them." At Genesis 2:4 Moses begins using the compound phrase *Yahweh Elohim*. It is the compound divine name that is used when describing the making of man in Genesis 2:7, the making or planting of the garden in 2:8, and the placing of man into it in 2:15. Reminding ourselves that Moses wrote Genesis as a sort of preface to the books of Exodus through Deuteronomy, using this compound name demonstrates an intentional shift to identify the Creator as the covenant Lord of Israel. The shift from creation at large to the creation of man then to man's Edenic vocation instills covenantal implications with what follows. If the covenant of works was revealed formally through the positive law of Genesis 2:16-17 and if the place of this revelation to Adam is the garden, then obviously *Yahweh Elohim* formally entered into covenant with Adam at that time and in that place. The explicit identification of the Creator as *Yahweh Elohim* does not communicate to Adam his vocation. Moses was not writing for Adam. Adam's vocation was revealed to him long before Moses wrote the book of Genesis.[4]

Consider the Words of the Prophet Isaiah

The earth is also polluted by its inhabitants, for they transgressed laws, violated statutes, broke the everlasting covenant. [6] Therefore, a curse devours the earth, and those who live in it are held guilty. Therefore, the inhabitants of the earth are burned, and few men are left. (Isa. 24:5-6)

---

[4] Because Moses' treatment is sparse in terms of what Adam knew about his identity (image bearer) and vocation (covenant of works), it could be argued that I am reading too much into the account. Let me address this briefly. First, my method of interpretation seeks to draw out of Moses' narrative what subsequent written revelation does. I am not imposing my thoughts on the narrative. I am imposing God's thoughts as recorded for us by the inspired words of Scripture writers. Second, it appears that Adam fell into sin relatively soon after being placed in the garden, certainly before Eve bore a child as far as we can know (see Gen. 4:1). It could be that Yahweh revealed more to Adam than Moses informs us about (or even knew) or he would have if Adam did not sin so quickly. Cain and Abel brought offerings to the LORD, but Moses does not tell us how they knew to do this (Gen. 4:3-5). Something similar happens with Noah (Gen. 8:20). The best way to account for this is that the LORD must have revealed more to those in the early history of man than Moses records for us.

The Scriptural Arguments for the Covenant of Works

The curse, which extends to the entire earth, came about due to "transgressed laws, violated statutes," and a broken covenant. Since the earth was cursed due to Adam's sin as our representative, Adam broke covenant with God in the garden of Eden and the effects of his covenant-breaking affects "those who live on the earth," that is, everyone. E. J. Young's comments support this interpretation:

> It must be noticed, however, that those who have frustrated the eternal covenant are not merely the Jews but the world generally. The frustrating of the covenant is something universal. For this reason we may adopt the position that the eternal covenant here spoken of designates the fact that God has given His Law and ordinances to Adam, and in Adam to all mankind.[5]

---

[5] Edward J. Young, *The Book of Isaiah, Chapters 19–39*, vol. 2 (Grand Rapids: Wm. B. Eerdmans Publishing Co., 1969), 155-60. See also John N. Oswalt, *The Book of Isaiah: Chapters 1-39*, NICOT, ed. Robert L. Hubbard Jr. (Grand Rapids: Wm. B. Eerdmans, 1986), 446, where he says: "While the eternal covenant may have specific reference to the Noahic covenant in Gen. 9:1-17 with its prohibition of bloodshed, its broader reference is to the implicit covenant between Creator and creature, in which the Creator promises life in return for the creature's living according to the norms laid down at Creation."

The Scriptural Arguments for the Covenant of Works

Echoing Young's words, "in Adam to all mankind," Michael Brown and Zack Keele say:

> For all mankind to be under such a covenant, it must be the same covenant God made with Adam as the father of all humanity. Isaiah, then, assumes the covenant of works in order to apply it to all fallen humanity.[6]

Here is a prophet, writing long after Adam was created and long after Moses wrote, utilizing principles that first started with Adam to explain the universal guilt of man. In this sense, Isaiah is very Pauline; or better yet, Paul is very Isaianic. This later text makes explicit what is implicit in an earlier text. This passage will be discussed under the next consideration as well.

Consider the Words of the Prophet Hosea

> But like Adam they have transgressed the covenant; There they have dealt treacherously against Me. (Hos. 6:7)

This text is disputed as far as its translation goes. The NASB's is the preferred one, in my

---

[6] Brown and Keele, *Sacred Bond*, 53.

opinion. The translation "like Adam" has a long pedigree, going back, at least, to Jerome. B. B. Warfield states that due to Jerome's translation, "to the Christians of the West it [i.e., Hos. 6:7] spoke of a covenant of God with Adam."[7] This is most likely why Muller asserts:

> The text indicated, as virtually all of the patristic and medieval commentators concluded, a prelapsarian covenant made by God with Adam and broken in the fall.[8]

This proves that the seventeenth-century covenant theologians did not invent the concept of a covenant with Adam, nor was the use of Hosea 6:7 as biblical support for such a concept

---

[7] Benjamin B. Warfield, "Hosea VI.7: Adam or Man," in *Selected Shorter Writings: Benjamin B. Warfield*, I, ed. John E. Meeter (Phillipsburg, NJ: P&R Publishing, Fourth Printing, January 2001), 117. Warfield's discussion is highly recommended for those interested in the history of the interpretation of Hos. 6:7. See also Bryon G. Curtis, "Hosea 6:7 and Covenant-Breaking like/at Adam," in *The Law is not of Faith: Essays in Works and Grace in the Mosaic Covenant*, ed. Bryan D. Estelle, J. V. Fesko, and David VanDrunen (Phillipsburg, NJ: P&R Publishing, 2009), 170-209; and Fesko, *Last Things First*, 88-91. Fesko agrees with Warfield that "like Adam" is preferred over "like men" or "at Adam."

[8] Muller, *PRRD*, 2:437.

The Scriptural Arguments for the Covenant of Works

novel. They stood on other's shoulders who pre-dated them. Warfield notes that the fifteenth-century Portuguese Jewish Bible commentator Isaac Abarbanel held this view, quoting him as follows:

> The meaning is that they have acted like Adam, or the first man, whom I put in the Garden of Eden and he transgressed my covenant.[9]

In the seventeenth century, Herman Witsius cited this text in support of the covenant of works, as did Wilhelmus a' Brakel and others.[10]

---

[9] Warfield, "Hosea VI.7: Adam or Man," 117-18. The quote comes from Husen's annotations on Abarbanel, cited as "Ed. Husen (Leiden, 1686), p. 270. Husen's annotations may be found on p. 282." Commenting on Abarbanel's view, Warfield adds: "The great name of Rashi may be quoted for the same view" (118). Rashi was an eleventh-century French rabbi who wrote commentaries on the Jewish Tanakh, what we call the OT.

[10] See Herman Witsius, *The Economy of the Covenants Between God and Man: Comprehending A Complete Body of Divinity*, 2 vols. (Escondido, CA: The den Dulk Christian Foundation, re. 1990), 1:135; Wilhelmus a' Brakel, *The Christian's Reasonable Service*, 4 vols. (Grand Rapids: Reformation Heritage Books, 1992, Third printing 1999), 1:365-67; Francis Turretin, *Institutes of Elenctic Theology*, 3 vols., ed. James T. Dennison, Jr., trans. George Musgrave Giger (Phillipsburg, NJ: P&R Publishing, 1992-97), 1.3.8

The Scriptural Arguments for the Covenant of Works

In Hosea 6:7, Israel is likened unto Adam. "But like Adam they have transgressed the covenant . . ." (Hos. 6:7). Fesko says:

> The most natural reading of the verse is a comparison between Adam, God's son (Luke 3:38), and Israel who is also God's son (Exod. 4:22-23).[11]

Warfield comments:

> No such exegetical objections [previously discussed by Warfield] lie against the rendering, 'Like Adam.' Any difficulties that may be brought against it, indeed, are imported from without the clause itself. In itself the rendering is wholly natural. Nor is it without commendations of force. The transgressing of Adam, as the great normative act of covenant-breaking, offered itself naturally as the fit standard over against which the heinousness of the covenant-breaking of Israel could be thrown out. And Hosea, who particularly loves allusions to the earlier history of Israel (cf. ii. 3, ix. 10, xi. 8, xii. 4), was the very prophet to think here of the sin of our first father.[12]

(1:576); and Ward, *God & Adam*. Ward's book is highly recommended.

[11] Fesko, *Last Things First*, 90.

[12] Warfield, "Hosea VI.7: Adam or Man," 128.

The Scriptural Arguments for the Covenant of Works

Warfield then cites Franz Delitzsch's comments on Job 31:33, where he cites Hosea 6:7. Delitzsch says:

> 'They have ['like Adam'] transgressed the covenant,' consists in this 'that Israel is accused of a transgression which is only to be compared to that of the first man created; here as there, a like transgression of the expressed will of God' (as also according to Rom. v. 14 Israel's transgression is that fact in the historical development of redemption which stands by the side of Adam's transgression).[13] And the mention of Adam in Hosea cannot surprise one, since he also shows himself in other respects to be familiar with the contents of Genesis and to refer back to it (see *Genesis*, pp. 11-13).[14]

Then Warfield cites Given from *The Pulpit Commentary*.

> *They like Adam have transgressed the covenant*: this rendering, supported by the Vulgate, Cyril, Luther, Rosenmüller and Wünsche, is decidedly preferable and yields a suitable

---

[13] Warfield has a footnote at this point which reads: "Hofmann, *Schriftbeweis*, I. p. 412." It looks like this comes from Delitzsch quoting Hofmann.

[14] Warfield, "Hosea VI.7: Adam or Man," 128.

sense. God in his great goodness had planted Adam in Paradise, but Adam violated the commandment which prohibited his eating of the tree of knowledge, and thereby transgressed the covenant of his God. Loss of fellowship with God and expulsion from Eden were the penal consequences that immediately followed. Israel like Adam had been settled by God in Palestine, the glory of all lands; but ungrateful for God's great bounty and gracious gift, they broke the covenant of their God, the condition of which, as in the case of the Adamic covenant, was obedience. Thus the comparison projects the shadow of a coming event, when Israel would leave the land of promise.[15]

Both Adam and Israel broke a covenant imposed upon them by God. They both disobeyed. They sinned, violating the covenants they were under. Both covenants were conditional, requiring the obedience of those in the covenant to enjoy the benefits of the covenant. As Moses says, ". . . in the day that you eat from it you will surely die" (Gen.

---

[15] Warfield, "Hosea VI.7: Adam or Man," 128-29. The Given quote is cited as "*The Pulpit Commentary*, on Hos. vi. 7 (p. 169)."

2:17; see Exod. 19:5-6 for the conditional nature of the Mosaic covenant).

Here is another prophet, looking back at previous written revelation, making explicit what was implicit in it. Remember, subsequent revelation often makes explicit what was implicit in antecedent revelation. The inspired words of the prophet give us God's infallible knowledge of similarities between ancient Israel and Adam. Both had a covenant imposed on them by God and both transgressed their covenants. Also, as with Isaiah above, the prophet's inspired words (e.g., in the case of Hosea, "transgressed" and "covenant") describe concepts first revealed by Moses, though in different words from Moses. As Brown and Keele say:

> Once more, the prophet's interpretation of Genesis 2-3 peeks through his prophecy, and it reveals that Adam was in covenant with God.[16]

If the interpretation of the Isaiah and Hosea texts is correct, either one or both of them, we have an example of the revelation of a covenant with Adam without the term being used to

---

[16] Brown and Keele, *Sacred Bond*, 54.

The Scriptural Arguments for the Covenant of Works

describe it in the Genesis account. The covenant with Adam is first revealed, though without the term "covenant" being used to describe it, then it is explicitly identified as such by subsequent written revelation. This same phenomenon occurs with the revelation of the Davidic covenant. It is first revealed without the word covenant being used then explicitly identified as a covenant by subsequent revelation. Let's compare 2 Samuel 7 with 2 Samuel 23 and Psalm 89.

"Now therefore, thus you shall say to My servant David, 'Thus says the LORD of hosts, "I took you from the pasture, from following the sheep, to be ruler over My people Israel. 9 "I have been with you wherever you have gone and have cut off all your enemies from before you; and I will make you a great name, like the names of the great men who are on the earth. 10 "I will also appoint a place for My people Israel and will plant them, that they may live in their own place and not be disturbed again, nor will the wicked afflict them any more as formerly, 11 even from the day that I commanded judges to be over My people Israel; and I will give you rest from all your enemies. The LORD also declares to you that the LORD will make a house for you. 12

"When your days are complete and you lie down with your fathers, I will raise up your descendant after you, who will come forth from you, and I will establish his kingdom. [13] "He shall build a house for My name, and I will establish the throne of his kingdom forever. [14] "I will be a father to him and he will be a son to Me; when he commits iniquity, I will correct him with the rod of men and the strokes of the sons of men, [15] but My lovingkindness shall not depart from him, as I took *it* away from Saul, whom I removed from before you. [16] "Your house and your kingdom shall endure before Me forever; your throne shall be established forever."''" [17] In accordance with all these words and all this vision, so Nathan spoke to David. (2 Sam. 7:8-17)

The "last words of David" (2 Sam. 23:1) are recorded for us in 2 Samuel 23:1-7. There David reflects on the account given to us in 2 Samuel 7. Notice what happens in verse 5 of 2 Samuel 23.

Truly is not my house so with God? For He has made an everlasting covenant with me, Ordered in all things, and secured; For all my salvation and all *my* desire, Will He not indeed make *it* grow? (2 Sam. 23:5)

The Scriptural Arguments for the Covenant of Works

David identifies what transpired as recorded in 2 Samuel 7 as the revelation of a covenant. The same thing occurs in Psalm 89.

> I have made a covenant with My chosen; I have sworn to David My servant, 4 I will establish your seed forever And build up your throne to all generations. Selah. (Psa. 89:3-4)

The psalmist evokes 2 Samuel 7, identifying a divine revelation of a covenant to David, though the first recording of that transaction is not identified explicitly as such. Meredith G. Kline notes this phenomenon while referencing Isaiah 24:5 and Hosea 6:7.

> Actually, it is possible that the Bible itself, in later references back to Genesis 1-3, applies the term *berith* [i.e., covenant] to the situation there, just as 2 Samuel 23:5 and Psalm 89:3 refer to God's covenantal revelation to David as a *berith*, though the term is not employed in the account of it in 2 Samuel 7. Isaiah 24:5 and Hosea 6:7 have been suggested as instances of this. Although the meaning of both passages is disputed, the everlasting covenant of Isaiah 24:5 definitely appears to refer to the

creational arrangements and Hosea 6:7 probably refers to Adam as the breaker of a covenant.[17]

Could it be that what occurs in 2 Samuel 23:5 and Psalm 89:3 also occurs in Isaiah 24:5 and Hosea 6:7? I think this is exactly what is happening. Narrative accounts of earlier written revelation are evoked by subsequent authors of Scripture, identifying in explicit words the concepts implicit in those accounts. The case presented above illustrates a pattern of inner-biblical interpretation. Later writers often pick up on former acts of God and explain what was transpiring in terms and phrases not used by the narrative accounts of those revelatory acts. We saw this happening with Moses in Genesis 2:4ff. In fact, this phenomenon occurs throughout the Old Testament. Earlier recorded revelatory acts of God are explained by later writers in words not used by the authors of the earlier recorded revelatory acts. Since the writings of the later authors are inspired, as the former, what we have is the divine explanation of the previous revelatory acts of God. And

---

[17] Meredith G. Kline, *Kingdom Prologue: Genesis Foundations for a Covenantal Worldview* (Overland Park, KS: Two Age Press, 2000), 14.

The Scriptural Arguments for the Covenant of Works

since we have a divine explanation, we also have an infallible interpretation.

Consider Why it is Denominated the "Covenant of Works"

It is called the "covenant of works" due to the fact that it was conditioned on Adam's obedience, or his works. The term "works" in the phrase "covenant of works" is a synonym for obedience. It is a term that reflects subsequent biblical, and therefore infallible, reflection upon Adam's Edenic vocation (see Rom. 5:12-21). Romans 5:19 justifies this term when it says:

> For as through the one man's *disobedience* the many were made sinners, even so through the *obedience* of the One the many will be made righteous. (emphasis added)

The opposite of "disobedience" is "obedience." A legitimate synonym for "obedience" is works.

The term works is also a good choice of words because it contrasts with "grace" and "gift" in Romans 5:17. Paul says there:

For if by the transgression of the one, death reigned through the one, much more those who receive the abundance of *grace* and of the *gift* of righteousness will reign in life through the One, Jesus Christ. (Rom. 5:17; emphasis added)

Adam's disobedience brought death. Christ's obedience brings life, a quality of life Adam did not have, i.e., eternal life (John 17:3; Rom. 5:21).

Prior to leaving this brief discussion on why the denominator "covenant of works" is appropriate, note well that, in this consideration and in the three following, there is a heavy dependence upon the words of the apostle Paul. The reason for this is that Paul often offers theological commentary on Adam's vocation, his disobedience, and the effects of his disobedience upon mankind. Commenting on Anthony Burgess' (a seventeenth-century member of the Westminster Assembly) method of understanding Genesis, Casselli says, "Burgess explained plainly that Genesis is only properly read through Paul . . ."[18] The apostle Paul takes center-stage in the writings of the

---

[18] Casselli, *Divine Rule Maintained*, 71, n. 140. We could extend this further by saying that Genesis is only properly read through the lens of the entire Bible.

The Scriptural Arguments for the Covenant of Works

New Testament as the one providing the most mature theological reflection upon Adam's vocation and the implications of it for mankind, Christ, and believers in Christ.

Consider the Fact that Adam was "a Type of Him Who Was to Come"

> Nevertheless death reigned from Adam until Moses, even over those who had not sinned in the likeness of the offense of Adam, who is a type of Him who was to come. (Rom. 5:14)

Let me first present some very brief comments on typology. First, a type is an historical person, place, institution, or event designed by God to point to a future historical person, place, institution, or event. An example of this would be the sacrificial system revealed to us in the Old Testament. That institution was designed by God to point to Christ's once-for-all sacrifice. Second, that to which types point is always greater than the type itself. For example, "the blood of bulls and goats" could point to Christ but could not and did not do what Christ's sacrifice did—take away sins (Heb. 10:4, 11-14). Third, types are both like and unlike their anti-types. The blood of animals was shed; the blood of Christ was shed. The blood of animals did not take away sins; the blood of Christ takes away sins. Fourth, anti-types tell us more about how their typical antecedents function as types. The blood of Christ takes away sins; the blood of animals pointed to that.[19]

---

[19] For helpful discussions on typology see G. K. Beale, *Handbook on the New Testament Use of the Old Testament: Exegesis and Interpretation* (Grand Rapids: Baker Academic, 2012), 13-25; G. P. Hugenberger, "Introductory Notes on Typology" and Francis Foulkes, "The Acts of God: A Study of the Basis of Typology in the Old Testament," in *The Right Doctrine from the Wrong Texts? Essays on the Use of the Old Testament in the New*, ed. G. K. Beale (Grand Rapids: Baker Books, 1994), 331-71 (The essay by Foulkes is exceptionally helpful.); James, M. Hamilton, Jr., *What is Biblical Theology? A Guide to the Bible's Story, Symbolism, and Patterns* (Wheaton, IL: Crossway, 2014); Paul M. Hoskins, *Jesus as the Fulfillment of the Temple in the Gospel of John* (Eugene, OR: Wipf and Stock Publishers, 2006), 18-36; Silva, "Has the Church Misread the Bible?," 57-61; Daniel J. Trier, "Typology," in *Dictionary for Theological Interpretation of the Bible*, gen. ed. Kevin J. Vanhoozer (Grand Rapids: Baker Academic, 2005), 823-27; Richard M. Davidson, *Typology In Scripture: A study of hermeneutical τύπος structures* (Berrien Springs, MI: Andrews University Press, 1981); and Leonhard Goppelt, *TYPOS: The Typological Interpretation of the Old Testament in the New* (1939; reprint, Grand Rapids: William B. Eerdmans Publishing Company, 1982).

The Scriptural Arguments for the Covenant of Works

It is important to note some specific considerations in light of Adam as a type of Christ. I agree with Bavinck, when he says, "Adam, the son of God [see Luke 3:38], was a type of Christ."[20] He was a type of Christ in his prelapsarian state (Rom. 5:14). Adam was a type of Christ as a public person (1 Cor. 15:22, i.e., federal or covenantal representation). Adam's failure is seen in the fact that he disobeyed or he failed to obey (Rom. 5:12ff.). He did not obey so he did not attain to the better state of existence to which the covenant of works pointed (more on this below). But what if he had obeyed? Would he have remained in the state in which he was created—able to sin and able not to sin? I don't think so and, I think, for good reason. And let me add that this is not an impractical, speculative, or abstract question, the answer of which cannot be known. It is a question related to the fact that Adam was a type of Christ. Let's explore this in more detail.

In Romans 5:21, God says, "even so grace would reign through righteousness to eternal life through Jesus Christ." The righteousness

---

[20] Herman Bavinck, *Reformed Dogmatics*, gen. ed. John Bolt, trans. John Vriend (Grand Rapids: Baker Academic, 2004, Third printing, July 2008), 2:562.

that is "to eternal life" comes as a gift to sinners and is based on Christ's obedience. The life-unto-death obedience of Christ constitutes a righteousness "to eternal life." In other words, according to his sinless human nature as the anti-type of Adam, Christ, our Mediator, earned eternal life for us. His righteousness was "*to* eternal life" (emphasis added). Guy Waters comments:

> The fact that Christ purchased eternal "life" for his own, and that he did so for those who were eternally "dead" in Adam means that Christ's work was intended to remedy what Adam had wrought (death), and to accomplish what Adam had failed to do (life). Paul emphasizes disparity in his argument precisely in order to underscore the breathtaking achievement of what Christ has accomplished in relation to what Adam has wrought. This means that if Adam by his disobedience brought eternal death, then his obedience would have brought eternal life. In other words, Christ's "obedience" and its consequence ("eternal life") parallel what Adam ought to have done but did not do. The life that Adam ought to have attained would have been consequent upon Adam's continuing, during the period of his testing, in obedience to all the commands set

before him, whether moral or positive. This life, it stands to reason, could be aptly described "eternal."[21]

Eternal life was earned by Christ, the anti-type of Adam, for us and given by Christ to us. The quality of life Christ attains for us and gives to us is not what Adam had and lost but what Adam failed to attain. Adam did not possess "eternal life" via creation. Robert Shaw, commenting on the covenant of works, says:

> There is a *condition* expressly stated, in the positive precept respecting the tree of knowledge of good and evil, which God was pleased to make the test of man's obedience. There was a *penalty* subjoined: 'In the day thou eatest thereof, thou shalt surely die.' There is also a *promise*, not distinctly expressed, but implied in the threatening; for if death was to be the consequence of disobedience, it clearly follows that life was to be the reward of obedience. That a promise of life was annexed to man's obedience, may also be inferred from . . . our Lord's answer to the young man who inquired what he should do to inherit eternal life: 'If thou wilt enter into life, keep

---

[21] Guy P. Waters, "Romans 10:5 and the Covenant of Works," in *The Law is not of Faith*, 230.

The Scriptural Arguments for the Covenant of Works

the commandments' (Matthew 19:17); and from the declaration of the apostle, that 'the commandment was ordained to life' (Romans 7:10).[22]

Just as Adam's disobedience brought upon him a status not his by virtue of creation (cp. Gen. 2:17 w. Gen. 3:8ff.; Rom. 5:12ff.; and 1 Cor. 15:22), so his obedience would have brought upon him a status not his by virtue of creation. Christ, as anti-typical Adam, the last Adam, takes his seed where Adam failed to take his. As will be argued below, Christ takes his seed to glory (Heb. 2:10), something to which Adam fell short.

Consider the Fact that Adam Sinned and Fell Short of Something He Did Not Possess via Creation

for all have sinned and fall short of the glory of God (Rom. 3:23)

In Paul's writings, it is clear that Adam was the first man who sinned. The first man sinned and fell "short of the glory of God" (Rom. 3:23), something which he did not possess or

---

[22] Shaw, *Exposition*, 124-25.

The Scriptural Arguments for the Covenant of Works

experience via his created status. As John Murray notes:

> [to fall short of the glory of God] . . . refers to a condition, not to an action, though, of course, the condition may arise from the absence of action which would have remedied or prevented the condition.[23]

Adam was not created in a condition or state that could be called "glory" and he fell short of it by sinning. He failed to attain that state because he sinned. In other words, Adam was created in a state that could have been improved, God being the ultimate cause and Adam's obedience the instrumental cause of the improvement. He was created in a mutable state, a changeable condition (2LCF 4.2). He was righteous, but he could sin. His obedience would have brought him to a higher state, an immutable state, conferred upon him by God due to his voluntary, condescending kindness expressed in the covenant of works (2LCF 7.1). Adam was not created with eternal life. Adam's obedience could have attained something with

---

23 John Murray, *Epistle to the Romans* (1959, 1965; reprint, Grand Rapids: Wm. B. Eerdmans Publishing Co., one-volume edition, 1984), 112.

The Scriptural Arguments for the Covenant of Works

which he was not created, "the reward of life" in the words of the Confession (2LCF 7.1). In other words, Adam had an eschatology before the need of soteriology. The soteriological strand of revelation comes because the eschatology of the garden was never attained by Adam. Or in the words of Geerhardus Vos, "The eschatological is an older strand in revelation than the soteric."[24] The soteriological (i.e., redemptive) strand of Scripture takes us to the eschatological (i.e., the goal) that was embedded in the protological (i.e., the beginning).

Because the subject of Edenic eschatology might be new to some readers, and is a debated issue in Reformed thought, let me take a brief excursus to demonstrate that what is being asserted is not new in the history of Reformed theology.[25] Take, for example, Nehemiah Coxe. According to Coxe, Adam had "the promise of an eternal reward on condition of his perfect

---

[24] Geerhardus Vos, *Biblical Theology: Old and New Testaments* (1948; reprint, Grand Rapids: Wm. B. Eerdmans Publishing Company, 1988), 140.

[25] For further discussion on the eschatological motif in the garden narrative in seventeenth-century Reformed theologians, see my *The Family Tree*, 90-106. In later chapters of that book I show the same motif in Geerhardus Vos and John Owen.

The Scriptural Arguments for the Covenant of Works

obedience to these laws."[26] According to Coxe, the tree of life functioned sacramentally as

> a sign and pledge of that eternal life which Adam would have obtained by his own personal and perfect obedience to the law of God if he had continued in it.[27]

---

[26] Coxe and Owen, *Covenant Theology*, 44-45. Coxe gives three proofs with discussion for the promise of a reward on pages 45-46. Later in his discussion, he says, "He [fallen Adam] could no longer claim a right in, or hope for, that reward which was promised on condition of his perfect obedience to the law of that covenant which God had made with him" (51).

[27] Coxe and Owen, *Covenant Theology*, 45. Coxe justifies this function of the tree of life as follows: "The allusion that Christ makes to it in the New Testament (Revelation 2:7). . . . The method of God's dealing with Adam in reference to this tree after he had sinned against him and the reason assigned for it by God himself [i.e., Genesis 3:22ff.]. . . . This also must not be forgotten: that as Moses' law in some way included the covenant of creation and served for a memorial of it (on which account all mankind was involved in its curse), it had not only the sanction of a curse awfully denounced against the disobedient, but also a promise of the reward of life to the obedient." Here Coxe is articulating Owen's (and others') view of the relation of the covenant of works to the Mosaic covenant. Notice that Coxe utilizes subsequent revelation to aid in the interpretation of antecedent revelation.

According to Coxe noted above, God sovereignly proposes covenants with men in order to bring them to an advanced or better state than they are in when the covenant is revealed to them and ultimately "to bring them into a blessed state in the eternal enjoyment of himself."[28] Adam, Coxe says:

> was capable of and made for a greater degree of happiness than he immediately enjoyed [which] was set before him as the reward of his obedience by that covenant in which he was to walk with God.[29]

According to Witsius, the covenant of works or nature or of the law (as it functioned in the garden), ". . . promised eternal life and happiness if [Adam] yielded obedience."[30] Witsius sees Adam in a probationary state and capable of arriving at a higher, more blessed state of existence. He says:

> That man was not yet arrived at the utmost pitch of happiness, but [was] to expect a still

---

[28] Coxe and Owen, *Covenant Theology*, 36.

[29] Coxe and Owen, *Covenant Theology*, 47.

[30] Witsius, *Economy of the Covenants*, 1:150. The covenant of works has been termed the covenant of creation, nature, and the law by various older authors. They all refer to the same doctrinal formulation.

The Scriptural Arguments for the Covenant of Works

greater good, after his course of obedience was over. This was hinted by the prohibition of the most delightful tree, whose fruit was, of any other, greatly to be desired; and this argued some degree of imperfection in that state, in which man was forbid the enjoyment of some good.[31]

The more blessed state of existence was

eternal life, that is the most perfect fruition of himself [i.e., God; this echoes the WCF 7.1], and that forever, after finishing his course of obedience . . .[32]

This promise of life flowed out of God's goodness and bounty, not out of any strict necessity.[33] God voluntarily condescended in the revelation of the covenant of works, offering a reward to Adam for his obedience. The garden of Eden, according to Witsius, was a pledge, a type, a symbol, both temporary and anticipatory of a better state yet to be enjoyed.[34]

---

[31] Witsius, *Economy of the Covenants*, 1:69; see also 1:123-24.

[32] Witsius, *Economy of the Covenants*, 1:73.

[33] Witsius, *Economy of the Covenants*, 1:76ff.

[34] See Witsius, *Economy of the Covenants*, 1:106ff., esp. 1:109.

The Scriptural Arguments for the Covenant of Works

In other words, protology is eschatological, or the eschatological is embedded in the protological. Adam had an eschatology that he failed to attain.

Let's get back to Romans 3:23. Listen to John Owen. Notice that he references Romans 3:23 in this quotation:

> Man, especially, was utterly lost, and came short of the glory of God, *for which he was created*, Rom. iii. 23. Here, now, doth the depth of the riches of the wisdom and knowledge of God open itself. A design in Christ shines out from his bosom, that was lodged there from eternity, to recover things to such an estate as shall be exceedingly to the advantage of his glory, infinitely above what at first appeared, and for the putting of sinners into inconceivably *a better condition than they were in before the entrance of sin*.[35]

For Owen, "the glory of God" here does not refer exclusively to what God *possesses*, but to what God *confers*.[36] The eschatological state,

---

[35] Owen, *Works*, 2:89; emphasis added.

[36] Murray mentions this view as one of four options. He describes this view in the following words: "to fail of the consummated glory that will be dispensed to the people of God at the coming of Christ." He cites 2 Thess. 2:14 and Heb. 2:10, among other texts. These texts will be

glory, is that *"for which . . . [man] was created."* The state of existence to which Christ takes elect sinners is "inconceivably *a better condition than they were in before the entrance of sin."* Christ takes elect sinners to a state of existence that is better than the beginning.[37]

Now listen to Paul in Romans 5:1-2, "Therefore, having been justified by faith, we have peace with God . . . and we exult *in hope of*

---

mentioned in our discussion below. Murray opts for a different view, however. See Murray, *Romans*, 113. Charles Hodge mentions the view advocated above though opts for a different one. He says: "Others again say that the glory of God here means that glory which God promises to the righteous, as in v. 2." See Charles Hodge, *The Epistle to the Romans* (1835; reprint, Edinburgh; Carlisle, PA: The Banner of Truth Trust, Reprinted 1983), 90. We will note Hodge's comments on Rom. 5:2 below. Sanday and Hedlam recognize the view advocated here in William Sanday and Arthur C. Headlam, *A Critical and Exegetical Commentary on the Epistle to the Romans,* The International Critical Commentary, eds. S. R. Driver, A. Plummer, and C. A. Briggs (1895; reprint, Edinburgh: T & T Clark, Fifth Edition, 1971), 84-85. They cite Rom. 5:2; 8:18 and 30; and 2 Tim. 2:10. John Gill seems to hint at the view above in John Gill, *Exposition of the Old and New Testaments*, 9 vols. (1809; reprint, Paris, AR: The Baptist Standard Bearer, Inc., 1989), 8:438.

[37] See Richard C. Barcellos, *Better than the Beginning: Creation in Biblical Perspective* (Palmdale, CA: RBAP, 2013), where I argue this at length.

the glory of God" (emphasis added). Charles Hodge says:

> It is a[n] . . . exultation, in view of the exaltation and blessedness which Christ has *secured for us.* . . . The glory of God may mean that glory which God gives, or that which he possesses. In either case, it refers to the exaltation and blessedness *secured to the believer*, who is to share the glory of his divine Redeemer.[38]

Likewise, John Gill comments:

> by the glory of God, is not meant the essential glory of God; not that which we ought to seek in all that we are concerned, and which we are to ascribe unto him on the account of his perfections and works; but that everlasting glory and happiness which he has prepared for his people, has promised to them, and has called them to by Christ, and will bestow upon them . . .[39]

---

[38] Hodge, *Romans*, 133, emphases added. See Murray, *Romans*, 161-62, where Murray hints at the view I am advocating. Sanday and Hedlam, *Romans*, 121, acknowledge a future transformation of "man's whole being" from the text of Rom. 5:2.

[39] Gill, *Exposition*, 8:449. See Douglas J. Moo, *The Epistle to the Romans*, The New International Commentary

We get glory, a state of existence, because it is conferred upon us, having been secured for us by Christ. This is why we can "exult in hope of the glory of God." Since justified, therefore glory awaits. This "glory" is that to which Adam fell short.

Consider the Fact that Christ, upon His Resurrection, Entered into Glory

The Old Testament spoke about the Messiah who would come, suffer (due to Adam's sin and us in him), and enter into glory. Consider these inspired and infallible theological reflections on the Old Testament.

> Was it not necessary for the Christ to suffer these things and to enter into His glory? (Luke 24:26)

> and He said to them, "Thus it is written, that the Christ would suffer and rise again from the dead the third day (Luke 24:46)

> "So, King Agrippa, I did not prove disobedient to the heavenly vision, [20] but

---

on the New Testament (Grand Rapids: William B. Eerdmans Publishing Company, 1996), 301-02.

The Scriptural Arguments for the Covenant of Works

·

kept declaring both to those of Damascus first, and *also* at Jerusalem and *then* throughout all the region of Judea, and *even* to the Gentiles, that they should repent and turn to God, performing deeds appropriate to repentance. 21 "For this reason *some* Jews seized me in the temple and tried to put me to death. 22 "So, having obtained help from God, I stand to this day testifying both to small and great, stating nothing but what the Prophets and Moses said was going to take place; 23 that the Christ was to suffer, *and* that by reason of *His* resurrection from the dead He would be the first to proclaim light both to the *Jewish* people and to the Gentiles." (Acts 26:19-23)

As to this salvation, the prophets who prophesied of the grace that *would come* to you made careful searches and inquiries, 11 seeking to know what person or time the Spirit of Christ within them was indicating as He predicted the sufferings of Christ and the glories to follow. 12 It was revealed to them that they were not serving themselves, but you, in these things which now have been announced to you through those who preached the gospel to you by the Holy Spirit sent from heaven—things into which angels long to look. (1 Pet. 1:10-12)

The Scriptural Arguments for the Covenant of Works

The Son of God incarnate both suffered and entered into glory, a glorified state according to his human nature after his sufferings via his resurrection and as a reward for his righteousness, which, according to Paul, was "to eternal life." In other words, Christ, according to his human nature, became what he was not at the resurrection, which was the beginning of his exaltation.

Suffering and glory is another way of saying humiliation and exaltation. Paul speaks of the Son's humiliation and exaltation in Romans 1:1-4 and Philippians 2:6-9.

> Paul, a bond-servant of Christ Jesus, called *as* an apostle, set apart for the gospel of God, 2 which He promised beforehand through His prophets in the holy Scriptures, 3 concerning His Son, who was born of a descendant of David according to the flesh, 4 who was declared the Son of God with power by the resurrection from the dead, according to the Spirit of holiness, Jesus Christ our Lord (Rom. 1:1-4)

> who, although He existed in the form of God, did not regard equality with God a thing to be grasped, 7 but emptied Himself, taking the form of a bond-servant, *and* being

made in the likeness of men. 8 Being found in appearance as a man, He humbled Himself by becoming obedient to the point of death, even death on a cross. 9 For this reason also, God highly exalted Him, and bestowed on Him the name which is above every name (Phil. 2:6-9)

The resurrection of our Lord marks a new phase of messianic lordship (see Acts 2:36). Commenting on Romans 1:4 ("who was declared the Son of God with power by the resurrection from the dead, according to the Spirit of holiness"), Murray says:

> The apostle is dealing with some particular event in the history of the Son of God incarnate by which he was instated in a position of sovereignty and invested with power, an event which in respect of investiture with power surpassed everything that could previously be ascribed to him in his incarnate state.[40]

Just as "according to the flesh" in verse 3 defines the phase which came to be through being born of the seed of David, so

---

[40] Murray, *Romans*, 10. See Moo, *Romans*, 47-51 for a very similar view to Murray's.

The Scriptural Arguments for the Covenant of Works

"according to the Spirit of holiness" characterizes the phase which came to be through the resurrection. And when we ask what that new phase was upon which the Son of God entered by his resurrection, there is copious New Testament allusion and elucidation (*cf.* Acts 2:36; Eph. 1:20-23; Phil. 2:9-11; I Pet. 3:21, 22). By his resurrection and ascension the Son of God incarnate entered upon a new phase of sovereignty and was endowed with new power correspondent with and unto the exercise of the mediatorial lordship which he executes as head over all things to his body, the church. It is in this same resurrection context and with allusion to Christ's resurrection endowment that the apostle says, "The last Adam was made life-giving Spirit" (I Cor. 15:45). . . . Christ is now by reason of the resurrection so endowed with and in control of the Holy Spirit that, without any confusion of the distinct persons, Christ is identified with the Spirit and is called "the Lord of the Spirit" (II Cor. 3:18). Thus, when we come back to the expression "according to the Spirit of holiness," our inference is that it refers to that stage of pneumatic endowment upon which Jesus entered through his resurrection. The text, furthermore, expressly relates "Son of God with power according to the Spirit of holiness" with "the resurrection from the dead" and the appointment can be none other than that which came to be by the resurrection. . . . What is contrasted is not a phase in which Jesus is not the Son of God and another in which he is. He is the incarnate Son of God in both states, humiliation and exaltation, and to regard him as the Son of God in both states belongs to the essence of Paul's gospel as the gospel of God. But the pre-resurrection and post-resurrection states are compared and contrasted, and the contrast hinges on the investiture with power by which the latter is characterized.[41]

Christ's representation in the state of humiliation started at his conception and ended at his death/burial. Upon his death/burial, because of his obedience to the point of death, God "highly exalted him . . ." (Phil. 2:9). The incarnate Son of God, according to his human nature, obeyed and suffered due to our sin. He entered into glory as a result of or reward for his obedience and he did both as the sinless last Adam, representing those given to him by the Father before the world began (Eph. 1:4). All believers in Christ will be transformed and

---

[41] Murray, *Romans*, 11-12.

The Scriptural Arguments for the Covenant of Works

conformed to that state of existence. Paul says our Lord

> will transform the body of our humble state into conformity with the body of His glory, by the exertion of the power that He has even to subject all things to Himself. (Phil. 3:21)

Adam failed to comply with the conditions of the covenant God imposed upon him and brought with that the ruin of the human race. He fell short of the glory of God, a permanent state of existence in God's special presence he did not possess via creation. But here is the good news—another came, the last Adam, our Lord Jesus Christ, who suffered then entered into glory at his resurrection, and who is the agent through whom many sons will be brought to glory (Heb. 2:10), who will also "gain the glory of our Lord Jesus Christ" (2 Thess. 2:14). Owen says on 2 Thessalonians 2:14, "'The glory of our Lord Jesus Christ,' or the obtaining a portion in that glory which Christ *purchased* and *procured* for them . . ."[42] Christ *purchased* glory for all he came to save. He did so as the last Adam. He suffered to

---

42 Owen, *Works*, 11:203; emphasis added.

satisfy the justice of God and his obedience unto death resulted in his exaltation, an entrance into glory, and all those who are his will enter into that same glory as well. The last Adam takes his seed where the first Adam failed to take his. Adam sinned, he violated the covenant of works, and he fell short of the glory of God. Christ did not sin, he perfectly upheld the stipulations of the covenant of works imposed upon him (precepts and penalties) and entered into glory as our fore-runner. Our Lord not only lived and died for us, his resurrection was for us as well (Rom. 4:25).

This is the covenant of works and this is why I think the 2LCF is correct to include this doctrine. It is a doctrinal formulation with ample scriptural (and historical) support.

The Scriptural Arguments for the Covenant of Works

5.

Conclusion

Moses, writing after the historical acts of creation, utilizes the covenantal name of God, *Yahweh*, while discussing Adam's Edenic vocation (Gen. 2:4ff.). Isaiah utilizes concepts that started with Adam to explain the universal guilt of man, while using the word "covenant" (Isa. 25:5-6). Hosea, looking back upon previous written revelation, makes explicit what was implicit in it. The prophet's inspired words give us God's infallible knowledge of one of the similarities between ancient Israel and Adam. Both had a covenant imposed on them by God and both transgressed their covenants (Hos. 6:7). Paul, while reflecting on Adam's Edenic vocation, contrasts the disobedience of Adam and its results with the obedience of Christ and its results (Rom. 5:19). The term "works" in the phrase "covenant of works" contrasts with "grace" and "gift" in Romans 5:17. Paul asserts that Adam was a type of Christ (Rom. 5:14). Adam sinned and fell short of the glory of God (Rom. 3:23). Christ did not sin (Heb. 4:15) and, upon his resurrection, entered into glory (Luke 24:46; Acts 26:19-23; 1 Pet. 1:10-12), a quality of life conferred upon him due to his obedience (Rom. 5:21). This is the life he confers upon all believers.

These scriptural realities, understood by the utilization of the hermeneutical principles of the Holy Spirit as the only infallible interpreter of Holy Scripture, *analogia Scriptura*, *analogia fidei*, and *scopus Scripturae*, led to the confessional formulation of the doctrine of the covenant of works.

Some deny this doctrine as formulated above and in the 2LCF. Hopefully this short book will challenge those who deny this crucial tenet to reconsider their views. It is also hoped that those who confess this doctrine will be strengthened in their resolve to defend and proclaim it.

In closing, since there was a covenant imposed upon Adam in the garden, are we to insist that it was designed to keep him (and his progeny) in the state in which he was created? If so, this would seem to imply that divine covenants (at least this one) are designed to maintain man in the condition in which they come to him. Is this, in fact, the way the biblical covenants function? I think not. It seems clear that biblical covenants are imposed on men to bring them to a better state of existence. Since there was a covenant imposed upon Adam in the garden, then it was so for his good, unto a better state of existence for himself and for all those he represented. Adam was created morally upright, yet mutable. He was not created in a state that could be called "glory," as indicated above. Because Adam sinned, he did not enter glory. But, there is hope! Our Lord is the last Adam who suffered and entered into glory for us and for our salvation. Understanding the covenant of works helps us better understand the vocation of our Lord and the gospel with more clarity and theological depth.

May this brief treatment promote further study and contemplation upon the things discussed and may it help readers come to appreciate, love, serve, and worship our Lord with more understanding and thankfulness.

Conclusion

For Further Reading

Baines, Ronald S., Richard C. Barcellos, and James P. Butler, editors. *By Common Confession: Essays in Honor of James M. Renihan*. Palmdale, CA: RBAP, 2015.

Barcellos, Richard C. *Getting the Garden Wrong: A Critique of New Covenant Theology on the Covenant of Works and the Sabbath*. Cape Coral, FL: Founders Press, forthcoming.

_____. "*Scopus Scripturae*: John Owen, Nehemiah Coxe, our Lord Jesus Christ, and a Few Early Disciples on Christ as the Scope of Scripture." *Journal of the Institute of Reformed Baptist Studies* (2015): 5-24.

_____. *The Family Tree of Reformed Biblical Theology: Geerhardus Vos and John Owen – Their Methods of and Contributions to the Articulation of Redemptive History*. Owensboro, KY: RBAP, 2010.

Barcellos, Richard C., editor. *Recovering a Covenantal Heritage: Essays in Baptist Covenant Theology*. Palmdale, CA: RBAP, 2014.

Casselli, Stephen J. *Divine Rule Maintained: Anthony Burgess, Covenant Theology, and the*

Place of the Law in Reformed Scholasticism. Grand Rapids: Reformation Heritage Books, 2016.

Coxe, Nehemiah and John Owen. *Covenant Theology From Adam to Christ*, Ronald D. Miller, James M. Renihan, and Francisco Orozco, editors. Palmdale, CA: Reformed Baptist Academic Press, 2005.

Denault, Pascal. *The Distinctiveness of Baptist Covenant Theology: A Comparison Between Seventeenth-Century Particular Baptist and Paedobaptist Federalism.* Birmingham, AL: Solid Ground Christian Books, 2013.

Fesko, J. V. *Last Things First: Unlocking Genesis 1-3 with the Christ of Eschatology.* Fearn, Ross-shire, Scotland: Mentor Imprint by Christian Focus Publications, 2007.

Girardeau, John L. *The Federal Theology: Its Import and Its Regulative Influence.* Greenville, SC: Reformed Academic Press, 1994.

Hodge, A. A. *The Confession of Faith.* 1869; reprint, Edinburgh; Carlisle, PA: The Banner of Truth Trust, 1983.

Muller, Richard A. *Dictionary of Latin and Greek Theological Terms.* Grand Rapids: Baker Book House, 1985, Second printing, September 1986.

Further Reading

Renihan, James M. "Theology on Target: The Scope of the Whole (which is to give all glory to God)," *Reformed Baptist Theological Review* II:2 (July 2005): 36-52.

Shaw, Robert. *An Exposition of the Westminster Confession of Faith.* Fearn Ross-shire, Scotland: Christian Focus Publications, 1998.

Vos, Geerhardus. "The Doctrine of the Covenant in Reformed Theology." *Redemptive History and Biblical Interpretation: The Shorter Writings of Geerhardus Vos.* Richard B. Gaffin, Jr., editor. Phillipsburg, NJ: P&R Publishing, 1980.

Ward, Rowland S. *God & Adam: Reformed Theology and the Creation Covenant.* Wantirna, Australia: New Melbourne Press, 2003.

Warfield, Benjamin B. "Hosea VI.7: Adam or Man." *Selected Shorter Writings: Benjamin B. Warfield*, I. John E. Meeter, editor. Phillipsburg, NJ: P&R Publishing, Fourth Printing, January 2001.